# DEV, LADY CHATTERLEY AND ME

First published in 1998 by
Marino Books
an imprint of Mercier Press
16 Hume Street Dublin 2
Tel: (01) 6615299; Fax: (01) 6618583
E.mail: books@marino.ie
Trade enquiries to CMD Distribution
55A Spruce Avenue
Stillorgan Industrial Park
Blackrock County Dublin
Tel: (01) 294 2556; Fax: (01) 294 2564

© Maeve Flanagan 1998

ISBN 1 86023 076 8

10 9 8 7 6 5 4 3 2 1
A CIP record for this title is available
from the British Library

Cover photo courtesy of the author
Cover design by Penhouse Design
Printed in Ireland by ColourBooks,
Baldoyle Industrial Estate, Dublin 13

# Dev, Lady Chatterley and Me

## A 60s Suburban Childhood

## Maeve Flanagan

*For Marion and Caitlín and in memory of Donal*

# CONTENTS

# 1

## GAMES

'Please Mr Murdstone Sir, please Sir, don't beat me.' My smallest sister was crying and screeching these words at the top of her lungs. She was doing as I had instructed her to do. She lay across my lap on her tummy. Her arms and legs were flailing wildly. She implored me not to beat her. I had my hand raised high up in the air. I brought it down to hit her bottom, letting it land ever so lightly. We were in the garage, playing one of the games I had invented.

Anybody earwigging at the garage door would have been convinced that a most unmerciful thrashing was taking place. My little sister was gifted at simulating bloodcurdling screams. We had another sister recruited too. Her job was to provide sound effects. I told her to beat anything in the garage which could make plenty of noise. She settled on a pile of old carpet. She walloped the living daylights out of it with a big stick.

My mother and father appeared, whitefaced. 'What's going on?' they screamed at me.

'Don't worry,' I answered. 'It's only a game.'

'What kind of a game is it?' they persisted. 'Why is Róisín screaming like that if it's only a game?'

I could see that they weren't going to leave without a full explanation. Róisín was only a tot. She wasn't good at talking. She wore dungarees a lot when she was tiny. I lifted her up by the criss-cross straps of her dungarees and I showed her to my parents. She grinned from ear to ear. For all she knew this too was part of the game.

'See,' I said to them. 'She's fine.' I motioned to my other accomplice to stop whacking the carpet.

'What sort of a game were you playing to cause all that racket?' They were still not convinced.

'We are playing David Copperfield,' I told them. My enthusiasm for the game was waning.

'And?' they persisted.

'David Copperfield, you know; it's on the telly. I am Mr Murdstone, David's stepfather. Mr Murdstone hates David. He flogs him. David begs him not to but Mr Murdstone will not listen. Róisín is David because she is the smallest. Cliona is beating the carpet to make the sound of the slaps, that's all.'

I hated when my parents interrupted my games. I hated having to subject what I had imagined to their adult scrutiny. It made what I had dreamed up seem so silly. My parents left eventually, reasonably satisfied that nothing too dreadful was happening to Róisín. I was free to resume my game but it took some time for the magic to be restored.

I liked inventing games. I liked playing them with my little sisters. Many of my games involved floggings, whippings and beatings. I was gentle in real life; in play I was evil and sadistic. My sisters conspired with me willingly. We had discovered *David Copperfield* on the telly on Sunday evenings. Hugh Leonard dramatised many of Dickens's novels for BBC. We watched them all. Poor little David Copperfield wormed his way into our hearts and went on to inspire one of our best games.

I had to be Mr Murdstone. I was the instigator of the game; nobody else deserved the starring role. A villain's part was always best; I could roar and screech to my heart's content. Róisín was especially suited to the role of David. She looked just right. Verisimilitude was all-important in the games I invented. Mammy cut her hair in a pudding-bowl style, and when Róisín ran her fingers through it, it stood at right angles to her little head. She looked just like the pictures I had seen in a book of the small boys who were sent up to sweep the chimneys in London when Charles Dickens was writing his novels. There wouldn't be any lip out of her either; she was only learning to talk. If there were any mishaps while the game was in progress she could never get me into trouble. Any coherent account of what had happened would be beyond her powers of speech. I just had to have her for my game, and so I cast her as my little David.

'Come here till I thrash ye, ye young cur.' I would roar this at Róisín and begin chasing her around the garage. That was her cue to run and to scream as loudly as she could.

'Bewitching Mrs Copperfield's encumbrance, so that's what they call ye, eh? I'll soon bewitch ye with a good thrashing.' I would follow Róisín as she ran. I would catch her by her little britches. Then I would sit on the big wooden tool box my father made, cue my other sister for sound and begin the thrashing. Róisín then would have to begin to whimper and plead: 'Please Mr Murdstone, Sir! Don't beat me; please, Sir, don't beat me! I'll be ever so good. I promise.' I coached her well. Her lines were word-perfect. Not bad at all for a toddler who could hardly talk. She even managed quite a decent English accent.

Mammy and Daddy were in the kitchen. Mammy was getting the tea, carving up the remains of the Sunday roast to serve it to us cold. I could hear the clinking of tea things. She would be calling us soon. My heart missed a beat when, from my vantage point in the hall, I heard her say to my father: 'Donal, do you think we should stop them?' The them to be stopped were my sisters and me, and what she proposed stopping us from doing was playing Mass. We played Mass for months one spring. We played in the hall – that was how they heard us as they got the tea ready. A parental veto on the great Mass game was imminent, and that wasn't fair. We had gone to such trouble in our preparations for these Masses.

We scoured the hot press and found old tablecloths and sheets for the priest and her altar boys. I was the priest and my little sisters served at my Masses. I selected the hall as our church, not so that my parents could spy on me, but because it was long and thin and a slight bit broader at the top near the hall door. This was the shape I had noticed most frequently in the churches we went to. Best of all, though, was that the evening sun on those spring evenings filled the top of the hall with light, just as light poured through the stained-glass windows behind the high altars in real cathedrals. We set up our altar under the glass panels of the hall door. I picked one volume of the *Encyclopedia Brittanica* as my missal and we found an old cruet set and poured vast quantities of very diluted malt vinegar into it as the altar wine. For hosts I sucked lots of Silvermints to a wafer thinness and these were given out at Communion time to our congregation, which was augmented by a selection of teddies and dolls when I ran out of little sisters.

The Mass was said in Latin then. I didn't have a word of Latin so 'jabber, jabber, jabber' I intoned in improvised Latin, using that half-singing tone I had heard from real priests. 'Wibbly, wobbly, wibbly, wobbly,' my tiny acolytes chanted back at me. Up and down the hall we processed that spring, genuflecting, blessing the teddies and the dolls and chorusing at the tops of our voices. We hadn't yet had a chance to get tired of the game and its future was in the balance. 'Ah, they're fine,' my father said, and I cheered inwardly and said Mass for a few Sundays more in my fantasy cathedral at the top of the hall.

When I did tire of the Mass game I searched for something equally stimulating and diverting. For a long time I failed to find anything. Boredom threatened until Easter 1966 dawned and the whole nation plunged into an orgy of commemoration of the Easter Rising of 1916. Ceremonies replaced the lessons at school and every night we watched Éamon de Valera on the news unveilng a plaque, laying a wreath or inspecting some guard of honour. I was intrigued by this man, so thin and so tall that he towered over everybody. He was partially sighted and an aide-de-camp led him as he performed his duties.

As I watched de Valera a plan formed in my head; this man would be the inspiration for our next game. Éamon de Valera would fill the gap left in our lives since we stopped saying Mass.

We set to work. We had to get the garden ready. We created a mini-Arbour Hill and Garden of Remembrance combined, as these were the places de Valera always visited. I broke off huge boughs from the lilac bush and fashioned them into the wreaths which we would lay on a mound of earth from which a little tricolour already flew. In the garage I found an old overcoat of my father's and I covered it with St Patrick's Day badges. This was my de Valera outfit and the badges represented the military honours I was awarded for all I had done to save the country as a young man in Boland's Mills. Of course *I* had to be de Valera. I was taller than my sisters and de Valera towered over everyone at the real ceremonies so to achieve realism in our garden rituals, I had to take the starring role.

I practised walking stiffly, my sisters half-pushing me, half-pulling me. One of them always linked me just as the aide-de-camp did on the news. But we never got very far. We always collapsed into helpless giggles and that gave us a new idea for an extra dimension to our 1916 game. When de Valera laid a wreath on TV everything seemed to go smoothly but we doubted that that actually happened. Surely leading an old partially-sighted man about must have entailed some dificulties.

'Ten paces from the back door,' my aide-de-camp sister would say to me, 'then sharp right, four more paces and you lay the wreath,' and off we would go. But my strides were longer than hers, I would pull her off-course, she would have to shout at me 'oh no, Mr President, they're the gooseberry bushes.' We would fall about the Garden of Remembrance laughing and never lay the wreath. The de Valera game lasted through the spring and summer of 1966 until we had done some serious damage to the lilac bushes and to everything that flowered in the garden. It ended when we became so sick of it that we could not bear to play it again and we had to cast around for another piece of pageantry to capture our imaginations.

We played in the garden when the weather was fine. We sat on the cement path under the diningroom window and chanted improvised words to improvised airs. That's when we were playing African tribeswomen. I saw the African women on television on *Radharc* documentaries. We couldn't play that game in the garage because these women lived in warm countries. I had seen the real women sing as they prepared their meals outside their huts. We carolled our own horrible din skywards as we prepared made-up meals. I gathered up great quantities of clay and added some water to make my version of an African woman's dinner. I sang as I stirred and mixed my clay to mud. I sang my African songs in my African dialect. My sisters prepared other courses. They sang as they toiled in the boiling African sun. We played this game only on the hottest summer days. We served the meal up on leaves that weren't quite as splendid as the gigantic banana leaves they had in Africa.

The African women farmed too. They sat in front of their huts beating sheaves of wheat to get grain for flour. So did we. We picked the longest of the wild grasses and sat in circles on the cement beating them with big stones. We crushed our grain with crude pestles and mortars and added water. We left our mush to bake in the sun. The results of our endeavours varied. We passed them off as loaves of bread sometimes; on other days they were our pottery. 'Tap, tap tap,' went our stones on the cement path. 'Lahie, lahie, lahie,' went our African chorus. The man next door to us stopped our African game. He was ill and couldn't endure our songs or our tapping stones.

Mammy and Daddy grew vegetables. Daddy brought cabbage plants home from town. The plants were small, wrapped in newspaper. A little root no bigger than a thread dangled through the end of the newspaper. The plants were droopy and dead looking. Even after Daddy planted them I was sure they wouldn't survive. They lolled in the newly dug drills. A small, darker circle of earth surrounded them after they were watered. As I said my goodnights to the garden after a long day's play I was sure they would die. But they did not. And those that the wood-pigeons didn't devour grew fine sturdy heads inside clusters of heavy green leaves. I wanted to garden myself but my parents weren't keen: they wanted all the space for their own produce. I ignored their objections. I railed off a tiny garden for myself and made small drills. This wasn't going to be a silly flower garden; it was going to be a real market garden – albeit on a diminutive scale.

The inspiration for my market gardening game came from what I noticed when I was helping my parents to weed the real garden: plants and weeds were very similar. Small weeds had a little thready root like my father's cabbage plants; strong weeds had a stout root like a parsnip or a carrot. Weeding was a thankless and boring job but it led to the discovery of another game. I stopped discarding the weeds as my parents instructed. I put them aside; I planted them in the little garden I had corralled off for myself. I dug fresh drills, planted my weeds in tiny rows, watered them at night from a battered kettle. In high summer my sisters built their huts in the garden. They took up residence in the huts with their friends. They ate all their meals out in the huts, from trays my mother passed out to them through the kitchen window. I kept the ladies who lived in the huts supplied with vegetables from my weed garden.

On the road where we lived a real vegetable man called. He stopped in front of the houses, opened the back doors of his van and weighed out carrots and potatoes. Out in the garden I was the vegetable man. I had no van; I travelled by bike. Like the real vegetable man I also carried a notebook. I kept a stubby pencil behind my ear. I kept a strict account of who owed what. None of these women were allowed to ask for tick. Sometimes the ladies gave me a cup of tea. As I sipped my tea I advised them what to do with bold or sick children. I also sold them some cabbage plants. I wrapped my weeds in swirls of newspaper like the parcels of plants my father brought home from town. The ladies in the huts paid me in hedge leaves. If we ran short of change we went to the nearby shop. The shop was a tree which grew up against the garden wall. Two of my sisters ran that shop. They squeezed themselves in between the wall and the tree. They parted the branches, poked their heads out and served their customers. At night they closed the shop.

They folded the branches back into a tree shape; they left their premises and went off home to their huts.

We played in the house too. Our favourite place to play was the stairs. The stairs was a doubledecker bus. The post at the bottom of the banisters was the bar which was at the end of the platforms on the old-fashioned double-decker buses. We swung ourselves on and off the bus by using this pole. There were no men on the bus. Only women and children, tons and tons of children. That was all I had ever seen on real buses. We didn't have enough people to stand for all the children we needed, so we brought all the dolls and teddies we could find. Each lady travelling on the bus had to have at least five children. Some of the children had to be 'handfuls'. The ladies on the bus didn't know one another, but they conversed anyway. That's what I had seen women do on the real buses we went on with Mammy.

The children were being brought to clinics to get 'needles.' They suffered from many ailments; some had scabs, others crooked eyes or nits. One bear or doll wore a caliper. The child with the caliper was never bold. We discussed the children's ailments on the bus at the tops of our voices. If we needed to discuss a painful treatment the doctor was likely to prescribe, we resorted to spelling. We threatened to give our boldest children to the bus conductor. The best part of this game was that it involved an element of competition.

The best players of this game were the women who could claim the largest number of seriously ill children, but they also had to have the most complicated and difficult lives.

I used to stand on the mat inside the hall door; the mat was the bus stop. I would hail the approaching bus. I would swing myself on to the bus with all my children. I would settle myself on a step of the stairs. The steps were the seats. I would sit in beside another lady and all her children.

'Four kids under five,' I would say to her. 'Sure I haven't a minute to myself.'

'Are they all yours, Mrs?,' I would ask my sister as I surveyed her brood.

'Yes, Mrs,' she'd reply. 'And I've nine more at home.' That would never do: she was in danger of outwitting me.

'Ah, sure that's nothing. I have three in nappies as well as all these.' Someone from another part of the bus would then pipe up: 'I have nine in nappies, Mrs.' The physical impossibility of the statements never bothered us. The only concern was to outwit the other woman on the scale of domestic responsibilities.

'I had four washes out this morning before seven. Had to, or I'd never have been out in time to bring this fellow for his needle.' I lifted my teddy son by the ear and showed him to the other woman. Women were always talking about washes. The most efficient women were those who had the biggest number of washes out earlier than anyone else. We played that game when we were still young enough to be terrified of injections. We dissipated our fears by having lots and lots of children whose complicated complaints would respond only to gigantic injections.

We discussed our sleep patterns on the bus too – just like the real women we knew. The lucky ones had only had a broken night's sleep the previous night; the real heroines hadn't slept for years. They appeared none the worse for their alleged sleep deprivation.

On and on we went trying to outwit one another. We pursed our lips when we spoke. We rooted in our big purses for the money for the bus fares. We knotted big knots under our chins in our headscarves. We imitated everything we saw real women doing on real buses. When we tired of the game we swung ourselves down off the bus by the banister's pole.

When I got too old for these games my little sisters continued without me. At tea time they nibbled their bread and butter into pram shapes. They held pram races across the teatable. They played new games in the garden. I could hear them from my bedroom. They still used their huts, but my weed garden was overgrown and forgotten. One evening I heard strange sounds. I went to the window. My sisters were playing with the boy from next door. He was carrying a huge wooden cross on his back; my little sisters were lashing him as he walked round and round the garden. It was Good Friday; they were having their own Via Dolorosa out there. For a few moments I was almost tempted to join them.

# 2

## GRANNY

Granny didn't live with us. She came on long visits. She
was my father's mother and a widow. She had no house
of her own. When she was a younger woman she was a
national school teacher. She taught all her working life
on Inis Mór, the largest of the three Aran Islands. She and
her husband taught together. They lived in a house which
was provided for teachers. They would have left that
house when they retired and bought one of their own.
That never happened. Granny's husband was drowned.
She continued teaching. She reared her large family on her
own. When she retired she left Aran for good. She began
her travels. She divided her year up into long visits to her
children and their children. That's how she came to spend
several months of every year in Stillorgan.

Granny was tall and thin. Her wedding ring could twirl
around her finger. She had a large, hooked nose and big
black eyebrows. She had blue curls. She didn't go out very
much. The hairdresser came to our house and gave her a
'blue rinse'. Winter and summer she wore heavy clothes,
long tweed skirts and a polo-neck jumper with a cardigan

over it. I always knew Granny was in residence by looking at our clothesline: large pink and blue bloomers flapped in the breeze.

One corner of the livingroom was hers when she stayed. A large armchair was its centrepiece. We never sat on that chair when she was with us. She didn't come down in the mornings until the fire was really blazing up the chimney. She put her huge black handbag on the floor beside her chair. She dipped into her bag during the day for pills, letters and photographs. Last thing at night she took it upstairs with her. There were shelves on one side of Granny's armchair. They stretched down from the ceiling and ended in three presses. The flat surface on the top of the presses was Granny's too. Here she kept her medicines, among them a tonic to give her an appetite. It was thick and green and sticky. Most important of all was her yellow and blue tin of Bisodol. Granny took Bisodol several times a day. When I got older I was allowed to make it. I sneaked a tiny sip for myself; I loved its minty taste. I thought it would be a good idea to save up my pocket money and buy my own tin one day. Then I could drink as much as I pleased.

Granny didn't drink tea. She took Nescafé made on milk. There was a catering size tin of Nescafé on the top of the presses beside the Bisodol. My aunt was very rich. She sent her these big tins, They were good value. They also allayed any fears my Granny had of running short. Granny was a dreadful worrier. Her biggest worry was that she would run short of something. She told me about the war and the rationing. The hardest thing to endure was the rationing of cigarettes. All the smokers were miserable then. A residual fear of running short of cigarettes haunted her for the rest of her life. Granny didn't shop herself; I went for her. I was never sent for twenty Aftons; it was always forty. These unopened packets were stacked up beside the Nescafé and the Bisodol and whatever tonic she had been recommended.

The most sacred spot in Granny's corner was reserved for her prayer books and her rosary beads. I had to be very quiet every day when she said her prayers. I also had to be quiet when she listened to the *Kennedys of Castlerosse*. I listened to the *Kennedys* myself. Together Granny and I discussed the doings of Mrs Kennedy, Peadar and Christy. Everything in Granny's corner was within her reach. She passed the days reading, listening to the wireless, smoking and talking. She had a team of small granddaughters to run and fetch anything out of reach, go to the shops, or make the coffee and the Bisodol.

When I was very young and hadn't started school I would sit impatiently every morning longing for Granny to get up so that she could talk to me. She told me about all my cousins. I hadn't met them. She rooted in her big black bag and pulled out photographs to show me. She read me snippets of their letters. She encouraged us to behave well by telling us parables in which our cousins were either very bold or very good. If she detected a quarrel brewing she quoted:

Birds in their little nests agree
And isn't it a terrible sight
When children of one family
Fall out and chide and fight.

She could spot a lie a mile off. She looked us straight in the eye and said, 'Oh what a tangled web we weave/ When first we practise to deceive.' Daddy drove Granny if she was going out at night to visit anybody. She had friends who worked for Irish Lights. If any of them were posted in the Dublin area Daddy drove her to visit them. Daddy cursed for weeks after they visited the lighthouse in Howth. It was a dark night in November and he had dreadful difficulty negotiating the narrow roads around the lighthouse in Howth.

Life picked up when Granny came to our house. People came to see her. My aunts came. People she had taught came too. I could never imagining visiting my own teacher when she was old. I found it difficult to imagine Granny ever was a teacher. She was too nice. Proof that she had taught spilled out in other ways. When I started school she questioned me closely about what I was learning. She didn't think much of my teacher's methods. She sent me out to the garden one evening. I was instructed to bring in as many small twigs as I could find. She told me to arrange them into bundles of ten. With this educational aid she took my arithmetic in hand. Granny was not going to leave my numeracy skills to chance.

Mammy wanted to build Granny up. She was too frail and thin. She fed Granny porridge with the top of the bottle on it. She made her egg flips. She put a tablespoon of brandy into the egg flip. Granny sat at the fire sipping her egg flip from a tall glass. Someone said tripe was very nourishing. Granny ate tripe, onions and white sauce once a week after that. Tripe was the most disgusting thing I ever saw. It was like a white rug. I saw a tray of tripe in the butcher's window long before Granny began to eat it, and I ran past the window in fear and disgust. She was advised to drink a few bottles of stout. They came from the pub in a big brown paper bag and she kept them in her press in the corner. Granny didn't like stout. She had been a Pioneer too for years; she was embarrassed. She gave me little sips. I told the teacher that Granny and I drank stout all the time at home. 'Do you?' she marvelled. Granny was mortified.

Even though she didn't go out, Granny knew all that was happening in Stillorgan. We brought her all the news. We told her the neighbours' business. She never forgot a single bit. When she came on her next visit she asked for an up-to-date version of the story. She asked about them when she rang us from other parts of the country. There was one woman we knew; she didn't go to Mass. That was the talk of the place. Granny always asked had she mended her ways when she came. She filled us in on the news of the other places. We knew what the neighbours did in Sligo, Tralee and Charleville.

My youngest aunt lived in Galway. She was single. She was very glamorous. She had all the latest clothes and a beehive hairstyle. She came to Dublin to see Granny. She floated around our house leaving clouds of perfume in her wake. She sang:

Put your sweet lips a little closer to the phone.
Let's pretend that we're together all alone.

My aunt went to dances. She bought my Granny huge birthday cards. They were padded and perfumed, too big for an envelope. They came in a big cardboard box. Granny had a supply of them in her big bag. If we were good she would let us look at them and sniff them.

If someone rang for Granny my mother and father didn't want her to stand in the hall as she spoke. One of us was detailed to run ahead of Granny with a chair. We were to settle her at the phone and disappear. Under no circumstances were we to listen to her conversation, but we could still hear her opening words. Granny was from Cork. She never lost her accent. It got stronger when she spoke on the phone. 'Hello Noreeeeen,' she would say to my aunt. We thought that was hilarious; we just called her Noreen.

I wrote to Granny and she wrote back. She sent us birthday cards with a pound note inside. She stopped when her grandchildren grew too numerous. I never grew out of Granny. I was too young when she died to have begun to see whatever flaws she had. Every time she was due on a visit my sister and I vacated our bedroom cheerfully and squeezed in with our little sisters. Our room was 'Granny's room' while she stayed; we never went into it until she left. I liked coming home from school when she was in Dublin. I told her all my news. She was shocked the day I told her the Irish alphabet had changed. We could use English letters and 'h's instead of *séimhiú* dots. Granny never got used to that change.

She went to bed in the afternoons for an hour. I counted the time until she got up again. I went to the shops for her on my bicycle. I brought back a birthday card for one of my cousins and the forty Aftons. One afternoon I was cycling home from the shops. I had a string bag on the handlebars of my bicycle. Granny's messages were in the bag including the forty Aftons. The bag became entangled in the spokes of the wheel and the corner of one cigarette packet was crushed. The cigarettes would be ruined. I was distraught; I couldn't afford to buy a fresh packet. I went home and explained to Granny what had happened. Two or three cigarettes were crushed; she could smoke the others, she assured me. She never said a word to my parents.

I had another grandmother. She seemed to be younger than my granny Flanagan. She was very active. She looked after geese, hens and turkeys on her farm. She asked me one day about my granny Flanagan:

'How's the old lady?' she said. The cheek of her I thought; my granny isn't old.

The telephone rang one September morning. I was thirteen. Granny was due for her long visit. I was looking forward to seeing her. She wouldn't be coming; she had had a stroke. She lingered for a week. My parents went to see her. She died a few days later. I wanted to go to her funeral. My parents said no. I was to stay at home and mind my small sisters with my other grandmother. I never forgave them for not letting me say goodbye to her.

# 3

## SEX

My mother had the right idea. When the funeral party adjourned to the Ormsby Arms Hotel she left. She had been to the funeral Mass, the graveyard and the meal in the convent chapel afterwards. She had paid her respects adequately to the nun who had died. The nun was my father's aunt. She was nice. I was sorry she was dead, but she was old. I would have liked to have left with my mother. I wasn't allowed. I had to go with him, she said. My mother was grown-up. She could do what she liked. I couldn't. I had to go with him and lots of people I didn't really know. My mother had the excuse of a home to run, meals to prepare. She told my sisters and me to stay, to stay and come home later with my father – whenever that might be.

My heart sank in the hotel as a second and third round of drinks were ordered. Bottles of lemonade and crisps were passed back to us in our window seat. We were stuffed after the meal; we ate them anyway to pass the time. My father slipped away from us into a world we did not know. The conversation grew loud and animated. We were forgotten. I wanted to go home and change into a comfortable pair of jeans. I wanted to loll on the couch and watch something silly on television. I was a teenager. I didn't want to be fed crisps and lemonade as though I were a small child.

Some mourners had trains to catch. The party was breaking up. My father, sisters and I went to the car. We crawled in evening traffic all the way from Eccles Street to Stillorgan. Those who had left the hotel to catch trains were as far as Mullingar and Athlone by the time we arrived at our house. My father was in a bad temper. He had wanted to stay on in the hotel; we were deliberately left so that he couldn't. Those he would love to have spent hours with weren't free either; they wouldn't meet again until someone else died. He drove in angry spurts when the traffic permitted. His jerky braking and clutching spun the crisps and lemonade around in my stomach. I wanted to go home and get sick.

My father slowed to turn in our gate. He started to swear. 'What's wrong?' I asked. 'Look at your man,' he fumed. There was an enormous lorry blocking the gate to our house. Then my father began to laugh. The lorry was tipping a load of gravel into our drive. Bags of cement were lined around the garden wall. The builder was struggling to push a cement mixer up the path. 'The builder', said my father through the laughs, 'I forgot all about the builder; good job your mother was home.' He waved a huge cheery wave at the builder. He rolled down his window. He called out to the builder, 'Did herself look after you?'

I had forgotten the builders myself. That was a big

slip-up for me: I had a vested interest in the outcome of the builders' labours. We were having the house extended; I was going to have my own bedroom. No more sharing with my sister. How could I have forgotten that? I had been dreaming of it all my life.

We picked our way across the little patches of drive-way which were left. My father spoke to the men. They were to begin work the following morning; this evening they were delivering only essential material and tools. All my boredom and irritation vanished – my sick tummy too. I couldn't contain my delight. The builder had one more little job to do before he left. He reached into his van and brought out a small, wooden sign. It had his name and phone number painted on it. Our neighbours would pass it every day. If they liked what he was doing to our house they could call him for an estimate. That's how my mother and father found him. The builder hopped back into his lorry. I looked at his sign. I gasped when I read his name. It was John Thomas. I closed the hall door quickly. I ran upstairs like lightning and threw myself onto the bed. I howled with laughter. John Thomas! Mammy and Daddy had employed a builder called John Thomas to build the new bedrooms. He arrived the same day as the nun was buried! That nun was the only religious person in our huge family.

A voice call to me from below: 'Are you coming down for some tea?'

'In a minute,' I shouted back. But before I could think of tea there was something I needed to check. I took off my shoes. I stood on the bed. I reached into the air-vent up on the bedroom wall. Yes, something was there; my hidey-hole hadn't been discovered – even after all these years. I pulled up a plastic bag. There was a raggy paperback in the bag: it was my well-worn copy of *Lady Chatterley's Lover.* I flicked through some pages: no, I wasn't wrong, right there on the page was:

'John Thomas! John Thomas!' and she quickly kissed the soft penis that was beginning to stir again.'

Mellors was the gamekeeper in *Lady Chatterley's Lover,* and he did call his penis John Thomas. Had my parents smirked when the builder introduced himself? Did they know? There were some D. H. Lawrence novels on the shelves in our house, but *Lady Chatterley's Lover* wasn't among them. Had it been there I would have discovered it long long ago when I was conducting endless research into all matters sexual. I wondered if they had a secret copy stashed away like I had. There was one sure thing: I couldn't ask them; my parents did not discuss sex with me or my sisters.

I lay down on my bed with my *Lady Chatterley's Lover* propped on my tummy. I laughed and I remembered. I could recall reading about this novel for the first time, the obscenity trial and the stir the novel had created because of its sexual explicitness. Once I learned that it was explicit I had to have it. I remembered all the trouble I went to to get my own copy, to sneak it into the house and then to find the time and the privacy to read it. I had forgotten about my *Lady Chatterley's Lover* mouldering away in the air-vent until I saw the builder's sign. I couldn't wait to tell my friend but that would have to wait until school the next day: that matter was too delicate to be communicated over the phone. Meanwhile, there was a face to be de-grinned, tea to be taken with the family downstairs, some of whom were likely to burst through the bedroom door any minute if I didn't go down soon.

I was a teenager when my father's aunt died. By then I had no need of sexually explicit literature: I knew all about sex. This was due entirely to my own endeavours. No adult had ever helped me to discover anything about sex. They appeared to be determined to keep me in complete ignorance. Because they were mean and unhelpful, I embarked on my own research. For weeks and weeks I worked on my very own sex project.

My research on the project was lengthy and painstaking. It was often frustrating. Ultimately I was successful: I outwitted the adults who conspired to keep me in ignorance. Further research was unnecessary after I read *Lady Chatterley*. Connie Chatterley's cavortings with Mellors the gamekeeper put the finishing touches to my knowledge. I had a sentimental attachment to the book, but its days in the bedroom were definitely numbered. Soon, the builder would drill through my bedroom wall. New walls, rooms and air-vents would materialise in the space above the garage. It would have to go. I stuffed it back into its plastic bag and put it into my schoolbag. I would drop it into a litter bin on my way to school the next day. I went downstairs and joined the family for tea.

'Where do babies come from?' Children tormented adults with that question all the time when I was growing up. I didn't like babies. They were smelly nuisances; every family had some. I couldn't have cared less where they came from. My mother went off to hospital one spring evening when I was seven. I thought she was sick. She had gone into Holles Street to have my little sister; I hadn't even noticed her altered shape. When I was finally told where babies did come from it left me unmoved. There was nothing thrilling about babies or bumps.

Something quite different had my attention. I couldn't put my finger on what it was: I felt it. It was an energy, a strange, heady surge which filled the air sometimes when adults gathered. There wasn't the faintest hint of it about when my mother and father were living their boring everyday lives with us. But the air crackled with it when visitors called. Then it affected my parents as well. The adults' eyes sparkled, they threw back their heads, they laughed in throaty, seductive gurgles and they spoke in code. I could smell it in the huge bundle of coats and wispy scarves I carried up to the bedroom when the visitors came. That's what I was interested in, not where dribbly babies came from. I wanted to discover more about this fabulous energy, this wonderful cocktail which could transform my mother and father. But I was merely on the periphery; I carried their coats. I buried my nose in the bundle of different fabrics, trying to sniff it all out.

My mother told me about periods, pregnancies and babies. Plumbing, boring body-plumbing I thought. She never said a word about how the baby came to be in its mother's tummy in the first place. I had a hunch that the baby's beginning was connected in some way with the magic I had observed when adults gathered. But my mother was cute: she was keeping all the good stuff for herself as long as she could. She didn't let a thing slip.

That's when I had to begin researching the sex project. I started, armed only with one word: sex. All that I wanted to discover belonged under one umbrella term: sex. My first port of call was the dictionary. I looked up 'sex'. 'Sex: the difference between male and female,' it said. That didn't throw much light on the subject. This research was going to take time. I would also need privacy and peace. There were plenty of books in the house: whether or not they could help I couldn't say. Might I have to trawl through every one? I pleaded to be excused from the family drives. I hated them. I was always car-sick. My mother relented finally when I promised faithfully not to burn the house down or spend hours on the telephone.

While my family discovered the delights of Powers-court Waterfall and Howth Demesne I sat in the dining room with the *Encyclopaedia Britannica*. The *Encyclopaedia Britannica* was on the highest of the diningroom shelves. I needed a chair to get the volumes down. I had hoped that consulting one volume might suffice, but one volume sent me to another and another. It would take several opting-outs from Sunday drives before I was sexually word perfect. What I discovered added to my confusion. There were boring tables analysing the ratio of male to female births in different American states. No good. The footnotes were better: they told me where I could find the juicier bits. 'Sex: see courtship: animal/ bird' said the footnote. I read how pelicans and cranes billed and cooed. No help. I read another footnote: 'sex: see deviancy/sexual'. Now we were getting somewhere! But then I got lost. 'The abominable crime of buggery,' I read. What on earth was that? I found a better volume.

The volume which had 'reproduction' in it had a clearly labelled diagram of a penis. I gaped at it. I couldn't believe how big they got. This thing was enormous compared to the little worm my best friend showed me when he peed in the garden. The diagram showed the penis in its flaccid state. It explained in prose which even I could understand how and when it became erect. As if to leave nothing to the imagination, stretching way out beyond the penis was a series of broken lines. The broken lines denoted how far it could extend. It even gave the number of inches.

I grew blasé. I didn't care if my parents returned and discovered me reading the encyclopaedia. Parents longed for children to read big fat books of knowledge. Just to be safe, I took a peep in the non-sexual pages. I was safe as houses: Shakespeare was in the sex volume too. As soon as I could hear my parents' car in the driveway, I would flick back to Shakespeare. Sunday after Sunday I researched the sex project. I built up a patchy knowledge. Soon I exhausted all the *Britannica* had to offer. The pages I'd consulted repeatedly fell open automatically at some entry to do with sex.

But I wasn't happy. I had found out what my mother hadn't told me. I did know how the baby got into the woman. There were vague hints in the encyclopaedia that all this was an exquisitely pleasurable business but it didn't dwell on this enough for me. My hunch about the wonderful currents which passed between adults had been right. Tingling sensations which I was beginning to feel in my own body, were they connected to it too? How long would it be before I might join the adults myself?

I had to build on what I knew already. I needed to continue researching the sex project. Reading was the key. There was a press in the dining room full of *Woman's Weekly*s. Granny read the serialised love stories in the *Woman's Weekly* when she came to visit. I dipped in as well, but not into the love stories. I read the Letters to Matron. More pieces of the jigsaw fell into place. I wanted too to savour something which would give me an insight into the interaction between men and women, the delightful preambles to lovemaking, and of course, a detailed account of the lovemaking itself. There was a little bit of this in Granny's love stories. Wasn't she the sly old thing? There were women in those stories who longed for passion. Only a little bit came their way, a small account of a bit of kissing. That's all we got. They got married at the end of all Granny's stories. That was the last we saw of them. Granny was happy with that; I wasn't.

I rooted through all the shelves at home. Canon Sheehan and William Carleton were dead losses; so too was Annie Smithson. *Mary Lavelle* by Kate O'Brien was better. I skipped through the pages looking for a bit of sex; I wasn't remotely interested in a young provincial girl's impressions of Spain or Spanish life. Suddenly, there it was, slap on the page, a bit of sex; illicit too: Mary was in love with the married son of her Spanish family. I lapped it all up. Could what the adults experienced hold a candle to what Mary experienced with her Juanito?

I kept going with my parents' books. Their covers were dull and uninviting; they promised little and delivered less. I checked them out all the same, ever hopeful of finding a little sexy gem. I browsed in bookshops. Eason's was the best shop: so many shelves of luridly covered paperbacks for me to flick through. I wished my parents were Harold Robbins fans; the gaudy covers of his books were just what I wanted.

I found my sexy gem. A circuitous route brought it to me. One day at home while rooting yet again through the shelves I came to a dull hardbacked book. I almost cast it aside. What took my attention were the old black and white photographs in it. This book wasn't a novel. I hadn't read any non-fiction before. The book was called *Portrait of a Genius*, the life of D. H. Lawrence. I never heard of the man. I dipped in. Most of the book went over my head. I did understand enough to discover that this Lawrence chap and his books caused a right fuss. And all because he was writing about my favourite subject. There had been a trial for obscenity: if I could get hold of the 'obscene' book, my sex research could finish.

I bought a second-hand copy of *Lady Chatterley's Lover* shortly after my discovery. I sneaked it home to what I considered to be an inspired choice of hidey-hole: my bedroom air-vent. The air-vent was damp and full of spiders. I didn't want my lovely book's pages to go curly. I wrapped it in a plastic bag. I Sellotaped it to the inside of the air-vent. I treated myself too to ten Major cigarettes, hellbent on being wildly decadent. I came home at lunch time when I knew the house would be empty. I lay on the bed, I read my *Lady Chatterley's Lover*, I puffed on a Major. Sometimes I only just made it back to school. I finished the sex research. I had all the information I would need. I had the nuts and bolts from the *Britannica* and the emotional and psychological bits from all the novels. I was like an athlete poised on the starting block before a big race, waiting for the gun to tell me to begin. Deep down I was terrified the gun might never fire. Compared to the girls at school I was a non-starter. I had boned up on the theory; I was ready to roll. The difficult part was only beginning.

# 4
—

## Primary School

I sat in my classroom. My seat was the last one in the row nearest the window. Women were rushing down the lane beside the school to ten o'clock Mass. I knew some of them. They were the mothers of girls in my class. Sometimes they called to the classroom door with a forgotten lunch or to take their daughters away early for a dental appointment. There was a woman walking along the lane in the opposite direction to the Mass-goers. A little girl skipped along beside her. They walked to the top of the lane, got into a black Morris Minor and drove away. The lady driving the car was my mother. The little girl she drove away with was my sister. I peered through the slats of the classroom's venetian blinds. The car was getting smaller. It disappeared from view. My mother and sister were gone; nobody had seen them. I was safe, safe this time at least, from questions.

There were girls in my class who kept a close eye on all the comings and goings in the lane. If they spotted their mothers going to the shops and if our teacher's back was turned they would venture a quick wave. If they saw someone else's mother passing they sent a series of nudges through the rows of desks to alert that girl to have her smile or wave ready. That was how they saw my mother. I did know she would be coming to the school to collect my sister to bring her to her weekly appointment with the child psychologist. I didn't tell anybody that she would be there. I didn't want to answer any questions about my sister. The questions came anyway when they were seen: 'Look, there's your mother; where's she going? Where's she taking your big sister? Why isn't she taking you too?'

I didn't answer. That didn't make any difference. It was only a matter of time before someone guessed, before someone put two and two together and worked it out for themselves. When that happened my life would become even more miserable and complicated than it was already. My sister was two years older than me. She was strange. I didn't know that until I went to school. My parents never told me she was different, never warned me that there might be problems. I was really keen to start school. When I got to school I was going to play with my new friends in the yard; I would go to birthday parties in their houses.

School didn't turn out that way; it was doomed before it began. Doomed because she had been there ahead of me for two full years. In those two years she had established herself as the school strange girl, the girl who was different, the girl who couldn't fit in. When I arrived I was only her sister. She had no friends. She couldn't follow the rules of any game; nobody picked her when they played:

In and out go saucy bluebells;
In and out go saucy bluebells;
In and out go saucy bluebells;
For she is the master.

*or*

Queenie eye-o, who has the ball?
Is she big or is she small?
Is she fat or is she thin?
Is she like a rolling pin?

The girls from my sister's class chanted and sang all these rhymes every lunchtime. But always without my sister. I didn't blame them. All she seemed capable of doing in the line of lunchtime playing was tearing up and down the steep grassy banks which bordered the schoolyard. Up and down she ran, every day, arms outstretched, lost in her own crazy world. She was making a show of herself, making a show of me. She would make a show of my little sisters too when they were old enough for school. If only she could be quietly different, I thought. Quietly strange, that wouldn't be too bad. But everyone knew her. They noticed her because she giggled and she laughed at the wrong times and she talked to herself.

I couldn't pretend she didn't exist: she was too loud and too obvious. I couldn't pretend we were not related: we had the same surname. Daddy drove us both to school together in the mornings, Mammy collected us in the evenings. Everyone had seen us together; trying to cover it all would have been pointless. I wanted to take her and shake her. I wanted her to see what she was doing to herself and to me. But she just giggled; she didn't understand me. She didn't know that those girls who laughed at her, who egged her on to do daft things, they were not friends. They were laughing at her, not with her. That made it worse.

If she carried on like that just to make me feel embarrassed I could have complained her to Mammy and Daddy. They would have punished her. That would have been the end of it. But to have had her in trouble just for being who she was would have been cruel. I wished my mother and father would come to the school some lunchtime; then they could see what was happening. I hoped that they might decide the school didn't suit her and take her away for good. I felt mean thinking like that. I longed for it to happen all the same. But Mammy was at home, too busy with my little sisters. Daddy was at work in his own school. They'd never be able to come. They said it was my job to look after her. If I let on things were out of control I would be in big trouble myself. I wanted to kill her for being so awkward, so different. I wanted to scream at the girls who jeered her in the yard: 'Stop, stop, can't you see she can't help it? Leave her alone.' What I wanted more than anything else in the whole wide world was to belong to another family, a family where everything was simple.

I sat in the shelters of the school yard listening to the wasps buzzing around the bins searching for the jammy lunch crusts. I was determined: I was not going out to play. I didn't want to be jeered because of my sister. I didn't want to hear her being jeered. I just wanted the bell to ring; I wanted lunchtime to end so I could go back to the classroom. The classroom was a safer place: she wasn't there.

My sister couldn't keep up with her lessons. Mammy and Daddy did them with her in the evenings. They repeated the catechism answers again and again: still she did not know them. They went through English reading, Irish reading, spellings and sums. When she understood a little bit they tried to add on the next bit. But it refused to stick. She cried when they got cross with her; she cried more when they slapped her. I cried when I heard their angry, raised voices. I cried for her and because of her. I wanted a real big sister who would play with me, fight with me, show me things and stick up for me. I didn't want to be the pretend eldest, minding this strange girl, terrified of what she might do next.

I was a nice sister to my little sisters. I didn't want to hide them. When I started school I showed them to everyone in my class. In the morning before I left for school I stuck my fingers in through the bars of my little sister's cot. She stuck a little fat finger to me, she twined it around mine as if we were wishing on the chicken's wishbone. She said goodbye in a toddler's lisp. She was beautiful. She had lots of freckles and curls. I played great games with another sister, Cliona, and I carried tiny Róisín around the garden on the carrier of my bicycle. I wanted to be a nice sister to my big sister too but too many things got in the way. She was everywhere; we shared a bedroom. She was ahead of me at school spoiling everything. I got all her old clothes. She failed at everything. I wasn't allowed to try in case I showed her up.

My sister's lessons were getting more difficult. Mammy and Daddy started to spend longer with her, trying to teach her. She giggled. They thought she was being bold. The pile of lessons grew higher. They slapped her more to make her understand better. They began each night with patience. They lost it. They changed to slaps. They argued about what they should do. They went on and on with the lessons; the youngest child in the house knew them before the end of the session. But she never did. She went to bed in tears. The lessons were not finished. She went to school the following morning. Her teacher beat her then.

One day there was a knock at our classroom door. I was wanted. A big girl stood in the corridor. I was to follow her. She brought me to my sister's classroom. The teacher stood at her desk. My sister was beside her laughing. The teacher was very cross. I had never seen anyone so cross before. Her ruler was on the desk on top of my sister's copy. She was shouting at my sister. She stopped as I arrived at the door. She crooked a finger at me. I moved into the room. The girls in the class were laughing. She pointed with her ruler at my sister's work. It was covered in blots; the answers to the sums were wrong. My sister had rubbed holes in the page. My sister smiled at me; she thought I was on a visit to the class.

'Would your father stand for this sort of thing in his class?' the teacher asked me. I knew he probably wouldn't but I wasn't going to tell her. I want you to go straight home this evening and tell him about this carry-on,' she continued. 'Woe betide you if don't, Miss.' The teacher dismissed me. The big girl didn't come back with me. I walked along the corridor to my own room. I wondered what to do. Disobeying a teacher was serious. Obeying her would be worse for my sister. I ran my fingers along the dusty tiles on the window ledge as I figured out what I could do. I wouldn't tell. If the teacher asked me I would say I had told. I would say my parents had sent my sister to bed with no supper, that we were all very sorry, that it would never happen again. The teacher couldn't prove I was lying, my sister wouldn't expose my lie: she wouldn't know what time she went to bed at.

Until the day the teacher sent for me my sister had just spoiled lunchtimes; after it she was in my classroom too. Everybody in my class had seen me being 'sent for.' Being 'sent for' meant serious trouble. My own teacher would have it all worked out too: she'd have me down as trouble as well. All the teachers were probably talking about us over their own lunches.

'What happened? Did you get the *bata*? Was it 'cos of your sister? 'Cos she's . . . well you know.' The girls in my class were madly keen to discover what had happened to me. It was sewing time in my class when I got back; that was how they could talk so freely. My fingers were filthy from the window ledge. I'd be in trouble with my teacher if she caught me sewing with dirty fingers. I was useless at sewing. I sat down and threaded a darning needle. The teacher had told us again and again not to sew with darning needles: the material we used when we were sewing was too fine. Darning needles poked huge holes in it. That day I didn't care: I didn't feel like sucking the thread to stiffen it and then squinting as I tried to poke it through the weeny hole of a fine needle. I had more pressing things on my mind. What if my sister's teacher kept sending for me? She could very easily: my sister was unlikely to get better at her lessons. What if my sister were kept back? Could we wind up in the same class?

I watched the girls from my class who jeered my sister in the yard. I remembered all their names. If they talked to me in the class I ignored them. When they missed their lessons I cheered inwardly; it was the least I could do for my sister. Some of the girls were very nice. I would have liked to be friends with them. They wanted to be friends too: they asked me to their houses after school. I refused. I had to. I could never have asked them back to my house. What if they heard Mammy and Daddy shouting at my sister when they were doing the lessons? What if they slapped her when my friends were there?

I couldn't ask them when the lessons were finished; the lessons never finished. They began at three o'clock. My mother sat my sister at the kitchen table. She stood at the sink scraping carrots and peeling onions. She called out questions to my sister. She pointed at the mistakes with her short wet vegetable knife. She dug the wet blade deeper into the page: the ink from the blue lines on the page swam messily into the writing. My sister didn't understand. My mother's eyes streamed tears, tears of temper, tears from the onions, tears of frustration and tears of sadness. Her voice rose. She leaned to the drawer under the sink. She reached for the wooden spoon. I ran out the kitchen door with my Enid Blyton and the quarter-pound of cough sweets I had bought on the way home – nothing on earth would have persuaded me to reveal all that to anyone from my class.

We walked home from school together. My sister stopped in every gateway. She stared in at garden gnomes.

She talked to herself. I could see people noticing her, adults and children. I kept well behind her. I quickened my pace as we neared home, made sure to be by her side as we approached our door. We had to pass the boys' school on our way home. The boys were even more cruel than the girls. They got to know her. They pointed her out as that girl, that girl who stared at gnomes and who stared at the shelves of pans in the breadman's van. A neighbour told my parents about her odd behaviour. My parents came up with a plan: I was to watch my sister closely on the journey home; if she did anything strange I was to tell. They would punish her. That could only involve more slaps. There was no other way to punish her; she didn't read, they couldn't stop her comics. She had a bicycle but she couldn't cycle it. I told on her only once: hearing her sob her heart out was enough to make me decide never to do it again.

The school doctor came to examine us every year. My parents had been waiting for ages for him to come and examine my sister. If the doctor agreed that she was strange, that school didn't suit her, he would write a letter. The letter would make an appointment for my sister with a child psychologist. She could come to him once a week. If she was a really serious case he would take her from our school and keep her at his clinic. She could go to school there. The doctor wrote the letter. My sister went for her weekly appointments. Mammy collected her from the school in the morning and she brought her back after lunch.

One day when my sister was in fifth class Mammy brought her to see him. This time she didn't bring her

48

back. I didn't know where the school was. She went every day on two different buses. She could talk to all the gnomes in all the gardens on her way to and from the school; I would never have to walk home with her again. Some girls asked where she was. Would she be coming back? Would I be leaving too? Horrible girls laughed. They said they knew where she had gone. Mammy said not to mind them. Said to tell them my sister was gone to a special school. I didn't bother. I knew perfectly well what 'special' meant. So did the girls. It was my mother who didn't have a clue.

She was forgotten about. Nobody ever asked how she was. Everybody was glad she was gone, especially her teacher. I was glad too: life was too difficult when she was around. I never settled after she left. I remembered too clearly how people who were trying to be nice to me now had jeered her when she was there. I wasn't prepared to trust them. My teacher read out my English compositions; I think she meant it when she said they were good. All I could remember though was the way she too had joined in laughing at my sister.

It was a very wet day. I forgot my wellingtons. Mammy sent my sister to my class with them. The classroom door burst open; in walked my sister. She didn't know she had to wait until she heard: '*Tá cnag ag an doras a mhúin-teoir.*' Neither did she understand to wait for the teacher to call out: '*Tar isteach.*' In she came. Up she went to my teacher's desk. She put the wellingtons on the desk. 'Mammy said you're to give these to Maeve Flanagan.' Off she went without another word. The girls burst out laughing. The teacher joined in.

I wasn't going to be won over by a few sweet words now when my sister was gone, far away, out of everybody's hair. This time I formulated a plan. If my sister could be forgotten so quickly and so easily by girls who knew her, maybe I could pretend she didn't exist. Every new person I would meet would know nothing about her. I was going to secondary school soon. My sister was staying at her clinic. In secondary school I would say I was the eldest in the family. It would be difficult to remember to say 'three' instead of 'four' when people asked me how many sisters I had. Mammy and Daddy would kill me if they ever found out what I was up to. But what if they never found out? If somebody called for me to the house and asked me who she was I would say she was a visitor. I would shoo them out the door quickly before it got too difficult. My plan helped me through the rest of the time in the primary school. Only a few girls from my primary school were coming to the same secondary school; I was nearly free.

# 5
—

## MY FATHER

Daddy had a lie-in every Saturday and Sunday when I was small. My mother used to send me up to call him. I would put my head around the bedroom door and peep in without saying a thing. I liked surveying the room first in private. After my mother got up my father stretched across her half of the bed. He dragged all the blankets with him and rolled himself into a surprisingly small ball. He seemed glad to have all the bed to himself. He could enjoy all the space and all the blankets too.

'Is she cross?' he would ask me sometimes. If I said yes he could bolt out of bed and be downstairs in seconds. I liked it when I got to the room and my father was still asleep. Before I called him I used to spend several moments peering through his glasses on the dressing table. I was fascinated by the two little bedrooms I could see through their lenses. In time I grew bolder; I tried the glasses on. I pulled them up and down the bridge of my nose. I tested the bedroom with the glasses, then without them. Glasses were fantastic; I was going to get some myself when I was older.

My father told us stories. The stories were silly. I stopped listening after I had heard the first one. But my little sisters called for them again and again. Every time my father said the words: "'I'll do it myself,' said the little red hen,' they fell about laughing.

Every morning my father ate bread and butter for breakfast. He never completely finished the piece of bread. He got up from the table, said goodbye and left for work. When I was too small for school I spent ages staring at his discarded bread and butter. There was always a row of tiny teeth marks left in the butter

My father did DIY. He made shelves, wardrobes, an enormous swing and a garden fence. I liked watching him as he worked. I loved the smells of wood, sawdust and paint. He asked me to help him. I passed him the tools he asked for; soon I got to know all their names. I was dying to use the tools myself but he wouldn't let me. 'Too dangerous,' he said. I had to be content with assisting. I sat on planks of wood as he sawed the other end. I handed him Rawlplugs when he was drilling. I caught the lovely curly shavings which fell to the garage floor when he planed wood. I could see that my teacher was telling the truth when she said paper was made from wood: the shavings on the garage floor looked almost ready to write on. Sometimes if my father wasn't about I opened the toolbox and had a little go on some of the tools myself. I had small bits of wood hidden away in the garage. I secured them into the vice. I planed away at them very inexpertly.

He warned me never to touch the chisel. I wanted to use it immediately. My father was wrong; the chisel wasn't sharp at all. I would show him. One summer Saturday he was making wardrobes in the big back bedroom. He had me with him helping. But I was bored; I was not stimulated by all this handing and holding. I wanted to chisel and saw and plane for myself.

'Dinner's ready,' someone called us from the kitchen. 'You go on down,' I said. 'I'll follow you; there's something I have to do first.' Off he went obediently as a child. For a smart man he was easy to fool. My mother would have known instantly I was planning something. The chisel was lying on the floor. I began to experiment with it. I had my wood ready; there was a little rectangle marked out in pencil. This area was to be gouged out with the chisel. I began to work. There was nothing to it, child's play really. But then it slipped. It was sharp. It nicked a fine slice out of the fleshy pad of my finger. It wasn't sore but it bled profusely. I would have to hide the blood. It the blood was seen my mother wouldn't let me help my father again. He would get into trouble for not having me come downstairs with him. I bandaged my finger with toilet paper. I went downstairs and ate my dinner.

'What's wrong with your hand?' asked Granny. 'Nothing,' I replied, thinking she had just seen the toilet paper. I raised my fork to my mouth. The blood had seeped through the paper; it was oozing down through my fingers, heading towards my wrist. I had to come clean on what I had done. 'Told you the chisel was sharp,' he said. He still retained me as his helper.

My father painted too. For painting he wore his 'painty clothes' and his 'painty glasses'. We begged him not to go out in these awful things. When he ran out of paint or turpentine in the middle of a job he refused to waste time by changing into clean clothes. He went off to Stillorgan dressed like that in spite of what we said. There was less for me to do when he was painting. Nonetheless I trailed him. I opened big tins of paint for him with the screwdriver. I stirred the paint with a long bamboo cane. I loved watching the paint thicken and swirl into its real colour.

My father didn't bring us up. That was my mother's job. He went to work every morning. At night he went to meetings. We dealt with my mother always. She called for my father only at times when serious discipline was needed. I hated that. He could be very cross at those times and that frightened me. He seemed to have a little system worked out for his dealings with us. If my mother wanted him to be cross with us he would be very cross indeed. That would stop us from troubling my mother again: she would leave him in peace. His life could carry on untroubled by children. I loved to help him with his painting, decorating and his DIY, but I learned to tread warily around him too.

My father had no taste in clothes. He had no sense of style. I wanted to change that. He drove a black Morris Minor. He hadn't noticed that Morris Minors had gone out of fashion. Indeed all black cars had disappeared. Multi-coloured Consuls, Corsairs, Zephyrs and Cortinas were what I could see in my neighbours' driveways. I wanted my father to buy one of these flashier models. These cars had a bench seat in front like a large sofa. I could picture myself on the bench seat beside my father as we cruised along. These cars had gadgets too: cigarette lighters on the dashboard and radios. I told my father about these new cars but when the time came for him to change the car he went off and bought another black Morris Minor.

My father was a national school teacher. That job had no glamour. Our neighbours were what their wives called 'higher civil servants'. They ran the country. They never came home before six o'clock in the evening. They carried enormous briefcases filled with important documents which children were not allowed to touch. They went away 'on business'. My father never went anywhere – except to school. I couldn't pretend to my friends that he was someone very important. We all went to school. We knew that teachers spent the day patrolling the yard, hearing the catechism and slapping the bold ones. His briefcase had the same books as my own little schoolbag; he even had a little plastic child's lunchbox. He drove in the gate every evening at half past three when the 'higher civil servants' were probably just finishing their lunches.

Our stylish neighbours wore dark suits. My father wore a sports coat. In winter he added a pullover. The dark-suited men carried white hankies in their breast pockets. The hankies were folded into a series of triangle shapes. The cloth triangles peeped out of the pockets like sharks' teeth. Some of the men wore rings and they Brylcreemed their hair. I decided that I would tackle my father about his appearance.

I broached my subject one Saturday evening. I was sitting on the rug in front of the fire. I had come from my bath and was drying my hair. I thought I would begin gently; I would mention only one improvement at a session. I settled on introducing my father to the wonders of Brylcreem. To illustrate my point I selected the longest and wettest strands of my hair. I combed these strands across my bare knee. They responded to my touch as I combed; they lay where I put them. My knee, I told my father, was just like his head. I was succeeding in coiffing my hairs effectively because they were moist. Mr So-and-So's stayed in place always because he wore Brylcreem. My father could have tidy sleek hair if he wore Brylcreem too.

Loud guffaws were his response. Huge guffaws into my face. My willingness to help him improve his appearance were spurned. There was no point in going on to discuss coloured cars, rings or pocket hankies. Jettisoning the sports coat would be out of the question too. He didn't want me as his style guru; he was grand the way he was. It never dawned on him that just because I was small that didn't mean I did not know about these things.

'Will you take a small Paddy with that?' my father asked me. He nodded in the direction of the pint of Guinness he had just bought me. 'No,' I replied. I couldn't mix drink. He could; he always took a glass of Guinness with a small Paddy.

We were sitting in the lounge bar of our local pub. Carrier bags from a gents' outfitters were lying on the seat beside my father. We had been shopping. Shopping for him. I picked; he paid. I was his fashion consultant. He was willing to take my advice. He had forgotten the Brylcreem conversation many years previously; I hadn't. It was difficult not to smile at the turn of events.

My father said he was colour-blind. If he wanted new clothes my mother went shopping with him. My mother loved clothes, loved shopping for herself. She looked well in all the outfits she chose. She didn't like going shopping with my father; she selected ghastly things for him. He didn't know what he was walking about in. 'They're a change,' she replied to me when I said it to her. Her lips were tightly pursed. 'Come shopping with me next time,' I said to my father. He agreed. 'I'll make you lovely,' I said to him as he backed into a space in Stillorgan shopping centre. He looked frightened. 'Not too lovely, please,' he pleaded. 'No,' I assured him, 'not too lovely.'

For years I shopped with him. We went to the pub afterwards. We drank the Guinness and the Paddys. We drank too much. We talked and talked. After each shopping trip he arranged his purchases on the bed. I matched the shirts up with the correct sweaters and trousers. He hung them in the wardrobe in that order; there couldn't be any mistakes in colours after that. We continued to shop after I left home. He would ring and book my services for a day in the holidays or some free day the school would have. He rang me one day. The eighth of December was approaching. Would I come shopping? 'I'm thinking of a navy blazer,' he said. 'That wouldn't be too much, would it?'

'Sounds grand,' I replied.

We did shop on the free day from school. We bought the blazer and lots of shirts to match. We went to the pub and we drank too much. 'Will you have another?' I asked him. It was almost impossible to buy him a drink. I stood up to go to the bar. I was very wobbly. 'Why not?' he said, 'a bird never flew on one wing.'

My father wore his blazer just a couple of times. He died the following December. He wore the blazer in his coffin.

# 6

## THE WOMEN'S LIBERATION MOVEMENT

When I was a child my parents bought the *Irish Press* every day. Time stood absolutely still during those years. Inextricably linked with that great lump of frozen and unchanging time is the *Irish Press*. Life in our home was calm, predictable and unquestioning. My parents sat in their armchairs, swapped pieces of the *Irish Press* and read bits aloud to one another. My mother loved Mab Hickman's cookery columns; she cut out all her Christmas recipes; she consulted them annually until, yellowed with age, they disintegrated.

Change came, unbidden and from an unexpected quarter; suddenly the routines and rituals we had always known were lost and gone forever. Mammy, Daddy and the five girls ceased to exist as a cohesive group.

The *Irish Press* began to feature a women's page. This was no ordinary women's page. There were no knitting patterns, recipes or handy household hints. This page dealt only with women's issues. It was edited by Mary Kenny and it hit our home with seismic force.

My mother rebelled; she underwent a metamorphosis.

She listened to the radio non-stop; she quoted Mary Kenny all the time. She praised Tim Pat Coogan; he was the most enlightened editor of all the daily papers: he employed Mary Kenny. She began to read *The Irish Times*; she added more names to her list of women to be quoted: Mary Maher, Mary Cummins, Nell McCafferty and Nuala Fennell.

Mammy was a housewife and a mother. She had been a housewife and mother for years. I thought she was happy; I was wrong, very, very wrong. She was deeply unhappy. She questioned the life she had been leading up to then. I shivered to think where her questioning might lead. Would she leave us? Was she unhappy with us or was this something all women were feeling? I did a quick mental zoom up and down the road we lived on; the other housewives were functioning in the usual way. It had to be us; we were making her unhappy. But that didn't make sense; we were behaving exactly as we had always done. In the days before the women's page in the *Irish Press* she was happy; we were happy. It was all Mary Kenny's fault.

I wanted the old mammy back, the mammy who cooked delicious Sunday dinners and made sausage rolls for tea. Mammy gardened. She drove the car. She wallpapered. She made jam. And then, out of the blue, she stopped. She stopped when Mary Kenny started her women's page. I hated that Mary Kenny; she was evil; she changed mammies. Because she changed mammies daddies also changed. Children had no choice – they had to change as well.

I didn't just miss my mother's lovely home cooking; there was a change in the atmosphere at home. That change frightened me. My mother and father now argued all the time and the arguments were bitter; they ran very deep. Before Mary Kenny and her women's page, they agreed about everything. I knew what to say to them; I also always knew what not to say. I felt safe then. Suddenly everything was different; a newspaper which had been part and parcel of our daily unchanging lives changed everything in one fell swoop. I didn't like newspapers then; their narrow little columns of print and no pictures were very boring. I was also too scared to check out the *Irish Press* for myself; there was something dreadful lurking on the women's page. I just had to take one look at my parents to see that.

It had something to do with words. Words like 'lib' and 'liberation'. These words flew like sparks in the tense atmosphere of our home. My mother and other women were not free. Men like Daddy had stolen their freedom; now they wanted it back. I wondered if all the men had come together and planned how they would steal the women's freedom. Would they steal my sisters' freedom when they were women? Would they steal mine too? What would my future be if that happened? I wanted to cover my ears and blot out all this awfulness; it kept bursting through in my parents' emotional exchanges.

Children's allowances were paid to men; married women who worked paid the highest rates of income tax; most people felt they shouldn't be working at all. Pubs wouldn't serve women pints; some women were even beaten in their own homes. These were terrifying revelations. I wanted to ask questions; there was nobody I could ask. If I asked my mother a question, she would have assumed I was on her side; if I asked my father a

question, my mother would have concluded I was on his.
They were horrible days. I hadn't known how happy I had
been until I became deeply unhappy. An idyll was being
shattered and there wasn't a thing I could do to save it.
The realities of the adult world were unfolding in a very
ugly fashion.

Women's liberation got a wider coverage; the *Late Late
Show* did several women's liberation programmes. By then
I was considered old enough to stay up and watch the
*Late Late Show* with the adults. My recent initiation into
adulthood delighted me. My finest hour had arrived; there
would be no more lying in bed, listening to adults laughing, or straining to catch just a little bit of the excitement
when the livingroom door opened and my mother left the
room during the commercial break to make the tea. The
*Late Late Show* was exciting; there was always a fuss or
a row. I had heard the adults discussing the bishop and
the nightie affair; now I could be a part of all that.

We sat down to watch the *Late Late Show* one Saturday
night. It was about my third or fourth *Late Late Show*.
Anxiety exploded in my stomach as the subject of the
programme was revealed: women's liberation. There in the
studio and on the panel sat all the women my mother
never stopped talking about. She went into raptures; my
father hit the roof. He picked up the newspaper; he
heckled the women from behind it. 'They're very shrill,'
he said from behind his pages. 'Why is it that when
women are in a discussion they won't let anyone else talk?
Can you tell me that?'

'Shhhh,' said my mother, 'can't you see that I'm
listening?' The tension in the room was palpable; I was

riveted by the drama on- and off-screen. I hoped that I would not be sent to bed if things got too hot and heavy – either in our livingroom or in Montrose.

Women's liberation was more interesting on the *Late Late Show* than in the dreary old *Irish Press*; there was a panel, studio audience, shouting, roaring and laughter; there were living breathing people debating passionately. Some of the women were very funny. Nell McCafferty was a mop of wild curls, reducing every anti-feminist viewpoint to absurdity and never stuck for words. All these women were confident and articulate; they buoyed each other up; the adrenalin flowed. It was difficult to make the connection between these wonderful creatures and my mother. But the connection was there; they were saying the very same things she had said. They were also sad, angry, even furious at the lot of women, but they were in it together; she had nobody. I listened more attentively to those women than I had ever listened to my mother or my father. My mother and father were only a man and a woman grappling fearfully with feminism and all its ramifications. These women were television stars; they had style; they went on protest marches; they carried banners. They were revolutionaries; they were afraid of nobody. They began to interest me.

I stole a glance across at my father; I was a little afraid he might have some sixth sense that another of his females was about to jump ship. He had his newspaper folded down to A4 size, doing the crossword, but he still had one eye on the television screen. He raised his eyebrows at me. I knew it was getting close to supper time. I signed a promise across to him that I would get it

in the next commercial break.

When the commercial break came I flew into the kitchen. My head was humming from all that I had heard. I cut big doorsteps of bread for my father. I'd stuff him with sandwiches; then maybe he'd fall asleep and my mother and I could watch the rest of the programme together in peace – if he didn't snore too loudly. I buttered the bread, sliced the cheese and slapped everything together at top speed. I didn't want to miss a moment of the programme. I wasn't angry with women's liberation any longer. I had even listened to Mary Kenny and she made sense. But then, wasn't it very easy to discuss a new idea in a television studio? Living with the idea in one's own home, that was the difficult part. Of course I could see the unfairness of women doing every single thing in the home. But when a woman discovered women's liber-ation and refused to cook the dinner, what happened then? What happened if her husband couldn't or wouldn't cook the dinner and their children were hungry and frightened? Or, if not cooking the dinner made the hus-band fight with his wife and she retaliated? That's what trying to change things in our house had done; the women on the television made it seem so easy and so attractive.

There was nothing I could do except go back into the livingroom and give my parents their supper. I would watch the rest of the programme and mull everything over as best I could, in silence. I was determined that no matter how confused I felt, I would say nothing. Saying things had got my mother nowhere; I didn't have a studio full of glamorous revolutionaries at my elbow to bail me out if I were embroiled in an unpleasant argument with my

parents. The television would be switched off after the *Late Late Show*, those magnificent women would fade to a little white dot and I would be completely on my own, more troubled than ever before. This women's liberation was infinitely more complex than I ever could have guessed but at least it didn't terrify me any more; my mother was not going mad.

I carried the supper tray into the livingroom; the Lyons Tea Minstrels were finishing their little dance. I had missed nothing. The *Late Late Show*'s downy owl re-appeared and we were off again. That programme set me thinking: in the weeks and months that followed, tiny new thoughts swam round and round in my head.

I had no brothers, Daddy was the only male in our house. My parents came from large families; they were sociable. We had a constant stream of visitors; I loved having visitors but there was one thing which I hated about some of these visitors. They looked into our livingroom, surveyed the family group and spotted one solitary male surrounded by six females. 'God, Donal, how do you manage with all the women? Do you ever get a word in at all?' Sometimes some of them would tweak our cheeks with their fat red fingers as they spoke. I always felt like crying when they spoke like that; I never knew why. After the *Late Late Show* and the new train of thought it had sparked off for me, I understood very clearly, all too clearly. The visitors were sorry for my father because he had only daughters, piles and piles of daughters. Daughters were not worth anything. The visitors breezed into our home, sympathised with my father for having only us and they tucked into the delicious food which my mother had prepared.

My father taught in a very big boys' primary school and he loved coming home to a house of girls. He said that to us many times in the privacy of our own home. But he never said it to these visitors. He could have put them very nicely in their boxes if he had; he never did and that was more hurtful than their crassness. Some of these visitors were our relations. Did that mean that even in our own family we were valued less just because we were girls? Did our father love us but at the same time not respect us? Could he combine both feelings? It wasn't just men who commiserated with my father because he had no sons; women did it as well. That shocked me. Could they not see what they were doing? Had they not yet noticed that in most households the man was the boss? He was the boss because he earned the money. When he came home from work at five o'clock his day's work was finished; his wife's day never ended and she got no pay. In many houses women and children skirted nervously around the man, precisely because he had the only power that counted – money. I could see why men might be keen to protect their own interests; for women to join with them as they did so made no sense at all.

My perceptions of my parents were shifting and sliding since the women's liberation *Late Late Show*. I began to look at other families in a different light as well. Every evening after school I went to play in friends' houses. We would spend hours playing happily in the long spring evenings. But as five o'clock drew near, a sadness crept over me. Our meals were ready and we had to go home. It was more than a sadness at a game being over. The daddy in whatever house I was playing in was due home; it was as if everything had to be different when he came in: all traces of frivolity had to be erased. None of these fathers ever explicitly demanded a patriarch's welcome; it was more subtle than that.

That time in my life became a time for decoding: decoding the subtleties, questioning the givens and analysing the 'always had beens'. When my mother went to town for a day she prepared our dinner before she went. We let it simmer dry and threw it out because she was not there to turn the cooker off or to serve it up to us. If one of our neighbours went to hospital to have a baby, my mother and other mothers carried trays of cooked food over to the woman's husband and children. Women like my mother who were beginning to demand their rights helped other women; their help ensured that the women's husbands did nothing.

Why, I wondered, wasn't every woman screaming? Why was it that the women who were screaming weren't screaming louder? Why weren't men shouting loudly too about all this injustice? Why did decent men like my father just mock them? And when the tiniest murmur rose from women about the injustices in their lives they were dismissed as lunatics, 'bra-burners' and 'man-haters'. There was a very dark side to all this clamouring for women's rights: I could scarcely bear to think about it. I had heard my parents talking quietly about *Humanae Vitae*; I had seen the television coverage of the contraceptive train, the jolly band of women who when they arrived back in Dublin brandished their blown-up condoms like balloons. But lurking beneath the party atmosphere of their foray into the North was the chilling reality of constant pregnancies; at some stage well into the future, might that become a reality for me as well?

I certainly had new-found perspectives and new-found knowledge but I could do nothing with them: I didn't have the power to live differently. I was only 'one of the children'. I never allied myself openly with my mother; I needed to protect myself from her just as much as I needed to avoid incurring my father's wrath. In the early heady days of women's liberation my mother sat glassy-eyed at the kitchen table. She always had the *Irish Press* splayed before her. I knew that she wouldn't have hesitated to use me to further her cause. I couldn't have lived with that: I loved my father too much. I had to learn to reconcile loving my father with hating his attitudes to women; that was painful enough without taking on my mother's problems as well.

My mother deserved my support; she needed it. She wasn't liberated. My father was a privileged man: he howled at the prospect of relinquishing even the tiniest shred of that privilege. I still didn't support my mother; I felt very guilty about that. I added guilt to the rage and hurt I was feeling. I carried on with my life – gagged, out in the suburbs.

The *Irish Press* continued to flourish; women's liberation was covered all the time on radio and television. My mother and her sister went to women's liberation meetings. My father complained; we children sulked. I moved into my teens. I became completely immersed in secondary school life. I still did not support my mother. I put a feminist gloss on my fear of taking a stand at home; if I prepared a meal to lighten my mother's load, wouldn't she be advancing towards her own emancipation at my expense? How would my mother square it with the sisters – handing her daughter the chains, the chains which she had just escaped from herself? What, too, if my parents' arguments weren't really about women's liberation at all? What if they were just projecting more deeply-felt disenchantments on to the women's liberation issue? If that were the case, I had no place at all in any of their exchanges. On good days my analyses formed a patina over a painful running sore; on bad days I limped along, close to tears but afraid to speak.

I expressed my true feelings about women's liberation just once. It was a wonderful and unexpected catharsis. It came my way in the form of the Intermediate Certificate Irish exam. Irish was the first paper we took. We sat in the school gym. The superintendent passed through the rows of desks distributing the question papers. The room was long; its ceilings were high. The glossy leaves of the convent horse chestnut trees glistened in the morning sun; the sky was vividly blue. We were sealed into the gym, in quarantine until 11.30. We were given our signal to begin and I turned my paper over. One of the essay titles was: *Cearta na mBan*. How could I not choose it? I, who had lived, breathed and suffered for women's liberation! I did that essay, and in doing it I tried to wreak a teenage revenge on all who gagged me; I wanted to settle a few scores. By this time I also had my knife in the Department of Education. The *Late Late Show* had raised my feminist consciousness; they discussed the role of education in reinforcing the traditional sex roles and nowhere was this more evident than in our Irish textbooks.

All through school we learned in Irish classes about what happened the day Mammy got sick. We learned the necessary vocabulary and then we wrote our own accounts of what happened in our own homes when our mothers got sick. These books operated on the premise that when a mammy got sick a replacement was needed on the domestic front; in those texts Mammy was always replaced by another female. Depending on our given linguistic proficiency, we wrote what we do, what we did, or what we might do; there was no escaping this part-icular scenario. It was always a Máire or a Síle who *scuab*ed the *urlár* and prepared a *dinnéar breá blasta* for a *Daidi*, a Diarmuid and a few Pádraigs. A series of wan little Cinderellas dragged hoovers across ugly schoolbook livingrooms; they carted trays up to their *Maimí*s in their *leaba*s; they beamed in gratitude when Daddy and the lads thanked them for the lovely dinners.

I was sick and tired of it all: our home, the rows and this nonsense in the Irish books. 'Glug, glug, glug.' I sucked a full barrel of ink into my fountain pen and I began. I couldn't have cared less about good or bad marks. I wanted to have my say, for once and for all, and with no repercussions. The anonymity of the public exam system was too good an opportunity to miss. I called for more paper; my friend glanced across at me in horror. 'Glug, glug, glug'; I filled another barrel of ink; there was no stopping me! As long as my *briathra neamhrialta* held out I would be fine. I had lived with Mary Kenny, the *Irish Press* and my parents; a few *briathra neamhrialta* were nothing to an old battle-scarred campaigner!

By the time I sat my Intermediate Certificate things had actually calmed down at home. We had not begun to do things differently. My parents had just tired of fighting; they had run out of steam. Life didn't go back to what it had been like in the pre-Mary Kenny days, nonetheless a calm prevailed. Cracks were papered over. Newspapers stopped publishing their women's pages: Utopia, apparently, had arrived. So many things had improved in women's lives the women's pages were no longer necessary. In future women's issues would be covered in the papers' main pages: there they could be savoured by the two, now equal sexes. Many married women, including my mother, returned to work. Every evening she prepared the dinner for the following day; she ironed each night until well past midnight. Rare flashes of her former indignation returned when she spoke of a neighbour she knew, some housewife whom she had seen in the supermarket handing back change to her husband. But the fire was gone; the crazy days were over.

Party politics were the real and final nail in the women's liberation coffin in my home; women's liberation ended as abruptly and as unexpectedly as it had begun. Long long before Mary Kenny my mother and father were in full agreement on one subject: politics. Their party was Fianna Fáil. They never had to worry about national politics: Fianna Fáil was always in power; they were free to fight the battle of the sexes; the country was in safe hands.

They emerged once and for all from their respective women's liberation bunkers when the Cosgrave coalition came to power. This was serious; this wasn't just women versus the patriarchy. They went into deep shock initially. A rapprochement took place; they came as close as they could in their combined hostility to the Cosgrave coalition.

It was not merely shock at the country's natural leaders being ousted, it was also the fact that the government was a coalition; the ship of state was headed for a watery grave; our very futures were hanging in the balance. Inter-party governments were inherently unstable; they always collapsed. They told us of inter-party governments that fell long before we were even thought of. We children were lost in a fog of names: Sean MacBride, John A. Costello and Noel Browne. People would begin to emigrate again, building would stop. Nothing ever got done when Fianna Fáil was out of power. I wished they would stop lecturing us about all this impending gloom. Secretly I thought emigration might not be all that bad: at least it would get me out of Stillorgan, where nothing ever happened.

My mother and father resumed their former positions in their livingroom armchairs; they swapped and shared pages from the *Irish Press*. My father no longer objected to it: the Kenny one was gone. Once again they read aloud to each other, any article at all, provided it outlined the more lurid deeds of Thornley and Cruise O'Brien. The country was in chaos; it was all hands to the pump time, and to argue if those hands should be men's hands or women's hands would have been the ultimate in treachery. Liam Cosgrave got my father off the hook; his electoral victory meant my mother came back into the fold and my father never had to change.

Women's liberation was never mentioned again. My parents battened down the hatches; they sat out the coalition years. My father was active in the local Fianna Fáil cumann working at national collections. He put up election posters and waited for the country to come to its senses. He was happy: this was real politics, not Kathleen and her feminist nonsense threatening to tear apart all they had started together when they married.

Nothing could ever touch me in quite the same way again. I was older and not so vulnerable, so too were my sisters. My parents could never channel that level of passion and hatred into any other 'ism'; there was no other 'ism' which could affect all our lives so deeply. Life really was better for my mother. She had money of her own and some help around the house from her daughters. She gave my father less grief precisely because she had money, choices and no more energy left. My father calmed down and we all breathed a sigh of relief: an aura of civility prevailed.

My parents got their wish: the Cosgrave coalition was hammered at the following election. Many of their most loathed TDs even lost their seats. Jack Lynch and Martin O'Donoghue romped home with their fourteen-point programme. My parents told us that we would never know poverty or emigration. That, combined with all the wonderful things happening for women – sure the world was our oyster!

The *Irish Press* is gone. Gay Byrne is silver-haired. The *Late Late Show* is anodyne. Mary Kenny has recanted. Nobody screams today, goes on protest marches or burns their bra. I am now the same age my parents were when they first discovered women's liberation. Mary Robinson has completed seven years in the Park. Many of my women friends are rearing young families. They wash, cook, clean and garden much as their mothers and my mother did. They have microwaves, dishwashers and their husbands have had 'the snip'. They are also holding down full-time jobs, but Biddy, not Miley, is advertising Surf. When women's liberation hit my home like a firecracker long, long ago it scared the living daylights out of me. It changed the country so very much and yet, in some ways, not at all.

# 7

## CHRISTMAS

Santa Claus was useless. I wrote to him every November, carefully describing what I wanted him to bring. He rarely got it right. He must have just glanced at my letter and forgotten what I had requested. Either that or he was forced to delegate some of the letter-reading to careless elves who failed to pass on the message. The latter was just possible; when I listened to *Letters to Santa* on Radio Éireann, the fellow Santa had helping him was a terrible eejit.

I wrote to Santa one year, asking him for a tricycle. There was a tricycle in my bedroom on Christmas morning but it was at my sister's side of the bed. The set-up in the North Pole was obviously every bit as unfair as the set-up in our home. I wrote to Santa the following year. I asked again for the tricycle. This time he brought me a scooter. Santa was getting closer; at least the scooter had wheels. I could travel on it but only in a very limited way.

I placed my right foot on the scooter's little tin platform. I pawed the ground with my left foot. The secret was in the pawing: the harder I pawed the longer I could travel when I put both feet on the scooter's platform. Meanwhile, my friends whizzed by me on tricycles; I was never able to build up sufficient momentum to propel myself after them.

Soon I was too old for tricycles. I wrote to Santa again. This time I asked him for a bicycle. A big two-wheeler, that's what I wanted. In my letter I told Santa I could ride a two-wheeler. I appealed to his thrifty streak: if he brought me a full-sized bicycle, he would never be troubled again by bicycle requests from me. I would keep it forever. I would keep it until I was as old as the ladies I saw in the country who bobbed up and down the lanes on black bicycles. They looked at least seventy. On Christmas morning there was a big two-wheeler bicycle in the bedroom: it was once again on my sister's side of the bed.

Santa Claus was supposed to know everything. He knew not to bring toys to children who were bold. If he knew that much, I thought the least he might also have known was my taste in toys. I didn't like dolls; it was my sister Emer who loved dolls and prams. Santa brought me a big doll. She was made of hard pink plastic and had curls and a dress. When I removed her dress I saw the little crying yoke glued into her back. It was a pink plastic disk with small holes in it. It looked like the little thing we had in the sink to catch the tea leaves. Santa brought me a cradle for her with a chiffon canopy over it. The bedclothes were frilly and flouncy, so too were the doll's clothes. I was supposed to spend many happy hours dressing and undressing this one. I could scarcely hide my disappointment the Christmas morning she arrived.

I wondered if it might be possible to remonstrate with Santa's representatives. These were the shop Santas we went to see in Clery's and Pim's. They usually asked children what they wanted the real Santa to bring. Maybe they had some influence. I lost my nerve when I saw one of the shop Santas. He had a scab on his hand. He asked me to sit on his knee but I refused when I saw the scab. He was only an ordinary man who cut his hand. He was nobody special and couldn't possibly have any influence on the real Santa. He was wearing a long red coat but a pair of ordinary men's shoes peeped out under the red material. A proper Santa would have worn a red jacket. He would have also had red trousers and black shiny fur-trimmed boots.

Preparations for Christmas began in our house after Hallowe'en. That's when my mother started her Christmas baking. The kitchen was stuffy from steaming Christmas puddings. My mother put the Christmas cake in the oven as she went to bed. It baked all through the night. She warned us not to open the oven door if we came downstairs at night. She wrote in lipstick on the oven door: 'Cake in oven, do not open.' If the oven were opened the fruit would fall. Whenever that happened my mother didn't give that cake away; it wasn't up to her standards. She cut it up and we ate it ourselves before Christmas. Fallen Christmas cake was nicer than successful cake, I thought. The top part of the slice was like madeira cake, but the lower half was crammed with fruit. It was delicious, all chewy and sweet.

Christmas cards came very early from nuns who were not allowed to write during Advent; they came early too from Australia. I watched for them every year, my early heralds of Christmas. My anticipation and longing might legitimately begin once they had arrived. I didn't like holy Christmas cards. The Divine Word Missionaries produced these, each one with Our Lady in a different pose. The cards I loved had to have big Santas, failing that anything with snow, robins or holly. There was a row about cards every Christmas at home. A packet of cards would arrive from the Disabled Artists in Cork. We hadn't sent for them. 'Bloody Disabled Artists,' my father would say, 'who gave them our address?' I was intrigued by this group who painted their Christmas scenes with their mouths and toes. I wondered what they would think if they heard my father giving out about them.

Newspapers, television and radio counted the shopping days to Christmas and I followed this countdown carefully. Shopping didn't concern me but the number of days left till the magic day did. I was too built-up for Christmas. It could never have lived up to my expectations. I had Christmas impressions formed from books, advertisements, sounds, tastes and smells. All these put together would constitute the perfect Christmas. All the elements from this mental collage would fuse together on Christmas morning. I would open my curtains and the world would be different. Everything I had ever dreamed of would be there, mine for the taking. I would surrender it all happily at midnight when Christmas would be over. But when the big day dawned it let me down; it was never grey and miserable – it just wasn't different enough from the other days.

We went to pantomimes, Jack Cruise in the Olympia

and Maureen Potter in the Gaiety. I hated the matinees. Children didn't listen; they bawled through the best bits. They went to the toilet. But if we went at night we drove out in the frost. I could see the plume of exhaust fumes on freezing January nights as my father started the car. When we drove through the streets I could see the neon signs, and there was a proper feeling of show business to the night performances. The theatre was red and gold. A man in a bow tie took our tickets. These things belonged to the night. The safety curtain was still down over the stage when we took our seats. It was grey and dull but the musicians in the orchestra pit were tuning up and they teased us into the magic which was to come. The instruments were mostly brass and when the musicians began to play for real, the sounds they made hit my blood. It never failed to happen. House lights dimmed, the music began, a long line of girls appeared. They wore glittery top hats, high heels and stockings. They danced their way across the stage; they kicked higher than I'd ever thought possible. Their eye make-up went over as far as their ears.

Every January I made a secret silly promise to myself: one day I was going to be on the stage. I didn't want to be one of those girls. I wanted Maureen Potter's job. I wanted to be a star. I wanted to enter after the dancers had warmed the audience up. I wanted to hold the audience in my power; I would decide when and where they would laugh or cry.

I didn't like the parts of the pantomime that were designed especially for children; the 'he's behind you' stuff. I wanted to see more sketches of Jack Cruise dressed as a woman, visiting someone in hospital, eating the grapes and scaring them with his discussions of diseases. I wanted a job which involved coming to the theatre every evening at six o'clock and changing into someone completely different. If that someone was outlandish and outrageous, so much the better.

Christmas was too long. Twelve days were too long to spend indoors in a house which was too hot. It was too long to go without seeing my friends. I got tired of watching my parents lounging in chairs, listening to Eamon Kelly on the wireless. Our lives were upended at Christmas. We went to bed late; we got up late; we gnawed turkey legs for breakfast. There were visitors every night. My parents brought them off to the sittingroom while we scoffed the sweets they brought as we watched Laurel and Hardy and The Marx Brothers.

The sixth of January was a holy day. The wise men were put into the crib. We went back to school, the bottles of milk didn't have holly on their foil tops and we had to remember to change the last digit when we were writing the date. When I walked home from school on our first day of the new year there was a desiccated Christmas tree at every gate. Christmas was great but I had had enough. We still had lots of cake to eat but the rooms looked clean and uncluttered without the decorations. My mother said she saw a stretch in the evenings. My father laughed; she said that every year. Soon snowdrops would try to poke their little heads above the ground. Spring was on its way. I was happy; my body was ready for light, heat and new things.

# 8

—

## BOOKS

The fire in the sittingroom had shrunk to red embers about the size of half crowns. The Christmas cards were buckled from the heat. I had been sitting by the fire all afternoon curled up in one of the big armchairs. My plan to spend ages and ages reading my new storybook had failed.

I felt cheated and cross. I liked getting storybooks for Christmas but the ugly thing on my lap wasn't a proper storybook. There were no pictures in this book; it didn't pop up either. I loved pop-up books. I would have loved another one but instead I got this book. Its pages were small; there were hundreds of them. Whoever had bought it for me said it was a wonderful book. I tried to make some sense of it, but the tiny lines of print defeated me. I even resorted to putting my fingers under the words, breaking them up into syllables and calling them out loud to myself. That's what the teacher did with the really bad readers at school. But nothing would come. I felt like throwing the book into the fire. It made me feel stupid. I stuffed it under the cushion of the armchair. I was determined to have nothing more to do with it. The book was called *Alice in Wonderland*.

I was upset because a book had disappointed me; I loved books. Reading time was my favourite time at school. I loved my English reader. There were beautiful pictures on all the pages. A boy, a girl and a dog had lots of adventures on the pages of my English reader. Billy, Lou, Pat and Toby they were called. They went to the beach for picnics. They made perfect sandcastles. Squiggly gulls hovered in the sky over them. There were five or six big, big words on every page. I could read them all:

'Run, Billy, run,' began the lesson. '"Look at me," says Billy, "I can run,"' it continued. It was all very simple. And that was the problem: the English reader was too simple, *Alice in Wonderland* too difficult. I was stuck in a 'no man's land'; nearly literate, but not quite.

Adults promised me that reading would come in time but adults were wrong about lots of things. I had caught them out and they could be wrong about reading as well. Even if I did learn to read, what if grown-up books were disappointing? All the books I saw adults reading looked just as boring as *Alice in Wonderland*. When I learned to read adult books I wanted to enter a world which was as exciting as the story in my pop-book of *The Queen of Hearts*. There was a huge page in that book; it showed the Queen's kitchen. She was at the table making her tarts. There were little flaps and tabs on the page. When I pulled a tab or lifted a flap another part of the story was told. One tab covered a mousehole; when I pulled the tab out a mouse popped, unknown to the Queen. And when I drew across the little flap I could see the maid out in the garden hanging out the clothes.

Our names were always written in Irish at school. The Irish alphabet was different. When my reading skills were imperfect I distinguished my Irish name from my English because it was much longer. The letter 'g' looked different too: it was beautiful. When we were taking our copies from the pile I looked for that 'g'. I also had to check that there were three other shapes after it. Checking for the three shapes after the 'g' was as important as looking for the 'g' itself: lots of other girls also had 'g's in their names.

We had boxes of crayons. The teacher wrote our names in Irish in joiny writing on the boxes. At drawing time I proudly located my own box of crayons. They were Finart crayons in a purple cardboard box. A small crescent shape was hollowed out across the centre of the box. When the crayons were packed properly in the box all their colours made a mini-rainbow.

A new girl came in first class. Her name was O'Reilly. She too would have a 'g' in her Irish name on her copies and on her crayons. But she was no use at reading; she couldn't even get the hang of Billy, Lou, Pat and Toby. But she did have confidence; oodles and oodles of it. Up she marched to the teacher's *cófra* when the drawing class began. She helped herself to my crayons. I told her they were mine but she wouldn't listen. I couldn't bolster my argument powerfully enough to get them back; my private method of decoding my name couldn't have withstood her confidence. Who was I to turn my nose up at somebody who couldn't master Billy, Lou, Pat and Toby, when I was only marginally more literate? I went back to my desk and

I watched her. She didn't open the box; she tore it. She ripped up the little crescent. She took the crayons; she broke them into smaller pieces to draw more easily. I sat in my desk and I longed for the day I could read properly – then I wouldn't have to suffer such indignities.

And one day it just happened. I could read. Anyone who could read was allowed to go to the school library. I found Enid Blyton and I forgot pop-up books. I ate, slept and drank *The Secret Seven*, *The Five Find Outers and Dog*, *Mallory Towers* and *St Clare's*. I wanted to go to a boarding school but I wasn't able to do my own plaits in the morning. I would have to postpone boarding school until Mammy showed me how to plait my own hair.

I didn't like the mysteries in the Enid Blyton stories. I preferred the descriptions of their picnics and all the ginger pop they consumed. I borrowed the Enid Blytons from the library, swapped the few I owned with my friends. I rarely bought any; an Enid Blyton paperback cost half a crown. I didn't have any half crowns to spare. It was silly to buy them too: they could be read in a day. I disappeared into a fantasy life where I played lacrosse. I went to midnight feasts in a dorm. A woman called Mam'zelle came over from France to teach me French. '*Tiens!*' she said to me again and again. I understood her perfectly.

When I got tired of Enid Blyton I had a dilemma: who was going to take her place as my favourite writer of all time? There were bookshelves at home in the diningroom. They stretched from the floor to the ceiling. I knew them intimately but it never occurred to me then that I might read them. They were part of the room just as much as any piece of furniture. I knew the colours of their spines, the titles, the authors; I would have noticed a gap when any of them were out on loan. I spent hours flicking through them on wet days. Some of them had been bought in secondhand shops. The names and addresses of their original owners were still written clearly on the flyleaves in copperplate handwriting. The books on these shelves weren't arranged in any particular order. But the alcove to the left of the fire was almost all Penguin paperbacks. There were shelves and shelves of orange and cream volumes. The oldest and most tattered had cost just sixpence.

The novels of Evelyn Waugh were on those Penguin shelves. A favourite pastime on wet winter afternoons was to take a look at them. I thought Waugh was a woman until I saw the small photograph on the back cover. He looked beautiful. He was blond and angelic. There were a few lines about his personal life too. The picture of Waugh was updated for the later novels; this time a more jowly Waugh appeared. He had married too. By the time I fingered through the volumes and got as far as those which cost three shillings and sixpence, Waugh looked ancient and he had six children. He had also become a Catholic. I traced his literary career and his personal life along our shelves. But I still hadn't read a line of any of the books at home: I merely ran my hands over them as a visitor might do with any ornament in a room.

There was a message in pencil in the margins of another book. The pencil was faded; the writing was dated sometime in the nineteen twenties:

If my name you want to see
Turn to page 133.

When I turned to the page as the voice had commanded
me I read:

Oh you fool, you cannot find it.
Close the book and never mind it.

I loved entering the spirit of that silly game. Whoever had
written it was bored and passing the time – just like me.
There was a name and address written several times too
and in the same handwriting: 'Josie Ryan, Charleville,
County Cork.' I asked my father about her. Granny was
from Charleville; her maiden name was Ryan. The scrib-
bler in pencil was his aunt Josie. She had died very young.
I was sad for days when I heard of this young woman.
She never had the chance to live her life fully. She never
dreamed that years and years after she had written her
little rhyme another bored girl would find it and smile at
her sense of fun.

I decided to approach the shelves in the livingroom
differently. This time I would tackle them with a view to
finding something to read. I was still looking out for
something to take Enid Blyton's place. I dragged chairs
and stools around the room to tackle the highest shelves.
I hurt my neck trying to read the names on the highest
spines. I pulled out each volume. I read a few lines and
if it didn't click with me immediately I put it back on the
shelf. That's what I did with Charles Dickens; his novels
were too long. I almost ran past Wilkie Collins's *The*

*Woman in White*, inside the cover there was a picture of a woman. She was wearing a flowing white dress. I thought she looked like a ghost. She would probably have given me nightmares.

One day I found something, novels by a woman called Annie Smithson. For a short while she replaced Enid Blyton as my favourite writer of all time. But there was a problem: we only had two of her books and according to the blurb she had written many, many novels. They were also out of print; apparently she was no longer popular. But my Kilkenny grandmother saved me. One day while I was visiting her and rooting in the presses I discovered she had the full set of Smithson novels. She let me take them all back to Dublin. The highest accolade I could accord this generosity was to address her as 'Grand-mother, dear', like Sheila in Smithson's *Sheila of the O'Beirnes*. She was touched; we beamed at each other across her kitchen, one Smithson fan to another.

I found a large hardback volume on the shelves called *Famous and Infamous Cases* compiled by a man called Patrick Hastings KC. I read about the trial of Oscar Wilde in this book. I neither knew who Wilde was nor why he was on trial. I read it because I thought he looked lovely. He had long hair parted in the centre and wore floppy ties. Wilde was in trouble. A horrible lawyer called Edward Carson was trying to get Wilde into trouble by asking him trick questions about whether he kissed boys. Wilde gave the lawyer smart answers; I didn't fully understand how they were smart, but when Patrick Hastings described the court's reaction to them, I had a sense that these answers were getting Oscar into deeper trouble. I cried bitterly when my lovely Oscar lost the case.

When I discovered a book I really liked I read it again and again. That habit was already in place before I started on our shelves at home. I read *Little Women* hundreds of times. I loved Jo March and I was angry with her when she didn't marry Laurie. I wanted to read the sequels and then one Christmas I was given *Good Wives* and *Jo's Boys*. I was disgusted with her when she married the ancient German professor.

By the time I got to secondary school I had had enough of the shelves and the library. I hadn't managed to find anything in either place which I really liked. My school textbook started me reading again. We had an anthology of short stories called *Exploring English*. We had a pre-scribed number of stories for the exam; our teacher didn't confine herself to them and any she didn't get to I read myself. We had school on Saturday mornings and I walked home the longest and slowest way, usually through the Stillorgan shopping centre. I started to visit the bookshop and it was there I bought my first adult book. Our teacher had read us 'First Confession,' by Frank O' Connor, from *Exploring English*. I thought it was marvellous. There were biographical notes at the back and they were marvellous too. If I liked a story it set me on the trail of the names of other books the writer had written.

In the Stillorgan bookshop I saw a Pan paperback called *An Only Child*. That was the autobiography of Frank O'Connor. I bought it and later found other collections of his stories and I added to my first purchase. I had a little cache of books in my bedroom but could only add to this when it was Christmas or my birthday. One writer led to another, O'Connor talked about O'Faolain. I bought some of his stories too. The second part of *Exploring English* was devoted to authors who were not Irish; there I found Saki and Katherine Mansfield. A writer whose name was new to me would appear in other contexts too: there were reviews in the *Sunday Times* and the *Observer*. Those reviews might speak of a book on Katherine Mansfield and maybe her relationship with Middleton Murry or her antipathy to Virginia Woolf. Because I knew one of the names, liked what I'd read, I was curious about the others. There was a logic to this discovery that my random rooting in the shelves lacked; it yielded more gems too. The lines of research were growing all the time. If I wanted to pursue them for ever it seemed as if there would be plenty of literature to keep me going.

I liked French at school. I was curious to see what the French might have written. On one of my visits to the Stillorgan bookshop I found *Memoirs of a Dutiful Daughter*, by Simone de Beauvoir. It was a Penguin paperback. Much as I liked French, I couldn't have read it in the original. Once I got into de Beauvoir I forgot about O'Faolain and O'Connor – forever. I cringed in teenage embarrassment and arrogance at my former tastes. How could I ever have been captivated by those provincials? Stillorgan wasn't large or sophisticated enough to contain me any longer. Cork and indeed Ireland were mere backwaters: I was off to Paris as soon as possible. I could just have been cajoled into accepting Bloomsbury as second best, but in Paris I would be able to breathe. I'd ramble along the Boulevard Saint-Germain, puffing on a Gauloise. I would tease out the finer points of existentialism with kindred spirits,

I am not a well-read or bookish adult. I read and re-read too many of my old favourite books for that to happen. There are thousands of books I will never get to. Books came into my life with the pop-ups. Billy, Lou, Pat and Toby initiated me into the rudiments of reading. They opened up new worlds when I felt hemmed in. They set me dreaming, soaring even, above and beyond a drab reality.

# 9

_

## PUZZLES

'That'll put a stop to her gallop.' That's what the adults I knew growing up said when they heard a young woman was getting married. The speakers of these words were mainly married women. They had a special tone when they spoke those words; it was gleeful and triumphant. They were experts on marriage. The prospective bride might well be happy, preparing for her big day with delicious anticipation that all her dreams were about to come true. My women knew otherwise. Their half-formed sentences and sketchy outlines painted a picture of life after marriage; marriage was grim and curtailed. The bride of the moment would be quoted. She was going to be different. The women's glee and triumph would then climax into a sneer: 'Oh, we all said that,' they'd reply and settle down to a cup of tea and some home-made scones.

I was very puzzled by their talk. If they knew the young woman was heading for disaster why did they not warn her? I would certainly try to warn any of my friends if I thought they were heading for trouble. They were dishonest too. They spoke only in private of the difficulties which marriage entailed; in public when a girl announced her engagement they congratulated her. They shopped for new outfits for the wedding, bought the happy couple a present and danced into the small hours with their own husbands in the hotel. If marriage was so difficult, I couldn't work out why they didn't go into mourning instead.

I didn't know many single people when I was growing up. Those I did know seemed to have better lives than the married couples. Single people came and went as they pleased; they could spend all their money on themselves. They had cars, lovely clothes; they went abroad on their holidays; they were always in good humour. Married people were short-tempered; they slapped their children on buses and in the supermarkets. Their hair was grey; they had varicose veins, no money; the children Holy God had sent them never seemed quite as nice or as well-behaved as those He sent their neighbours.

'When is the big day?'; 'When are you giving us a day out?'; 'Are you thinking of settling down?' Married people asked single people these questions all the time. They discussed them in private; they wondered how long more they might withstand the charms of marriage. At funerals, the saddest tone was reserved for: 'And she never married.' They caught up on news of people long gone abroad; here as well, the main focus of their attention was whether she 'ever married'. Marriage had a cut-off point; this was an age which was never actually mentioned aloud. There was a consensus of opinion that once this age was reached marriage was unlikely. I learned to recognise the imminent cut-off point. The tone of the questionings became more feverish; then they peaked and slid into a lament: 'Ah, she'll never marry now.'

I wanted to know why adults poked their noses so much into other adults' private business. Why were they so keen to get everybody married when in private they were candid about marriage and all its limitations? I couldn't ask; adults hated any questions which focused on their inconsistencies. Marriage was a subject strictly off limits to children; it was discussed by women when there were no children about. If they had nowhere to send their children they dropped their voices; the only information a curious child could glean about marriage was by eavesdropping.

One day the penny dropped. I wasn't puzzled any longer. Married people felt trapped; they had freely constructed their own elaborate traps and that made them mean. The only pleasure left to them was to see everyone else in a trap also. They envied the single people floating freely; they longed for them to feel as constrained as they felt. If many people were feeling frustrated, their own frustrations might seem easier to bear. If things worked out well, some of the forthcoming marriages might be absolutely awful; their marriage might begin to look better. That had to be the answer; it was the only one I could find to account for the adults' strange behaviour.

It also solved other puzzles. Couples who had no children were pitied; mothers and fathers with lots and lots of children appeared to wish they had none. Parents with children had ulcers, furrowed brows and empty wallets; people with no children had tidy tranquil homes. The woman kept on her job; they had time, money and energy to do interesting things. Pity merely masked envy.

Men did not discuss marriage as frequently as women. Sometimes they let things slip which showed that they thought similarly. When I was in secondary school our English teacher set us a difficult homework assignment; the question was on some complex aspect of our course novel. Our teacher was a single woman; she was also very formidable and none of us was keen to look foolish. One girl in the class was undaunted by the assignment. She would ask her father to help her; he had always been tops at English at school she claimed. When the teacher returned the marked assignments to us she was withering in her assessment of our classmate's father's school of literary criticism. The girl was mortified. He had been full sure that our teacher would be very impressed with his views. 'Did you tell him? What did he say?' we all asked her the next morning. I was concerned that he might not have survived the teacher's contempt. Not a bit of it! With a big grin she told us his reaction: 'What that one wants,' he said, 'is a few kids to quieten her.'

I was horrified. It wasn't only women who saw marriage and children as the end of their freedom; men thought it as well. They just said it less frequently. There was no mistaking what my classmate's father thought. I didn't like my teacher; I liked what that man had said even less. If the teacher had children she would 'be quiet'. She wouldn't have time to think about literature, have an opinion on it, or even dream of voicing her views.

'She's made her bed, let her lie on it.'; 'That'll put a stop to her gallop.' Ugly words abounded about marriage. Single young men and women were beautiful and un-

fettered. They did 'gallop'. They 'galloped' and 'galli-
vanted' great distances across the countryside following
their favourite showbands; they danced the 'Hucklebuck'
with whatever boy or girl they fancied. Married couples
glowered in housing estates; they wished a speedy end
to the freedom of the singles. They grilled them nonstop
about marriage plans. They wanted them side by side with
them in their rut.

I would have liked a nicer answer to my puzzles.

# 10

## SUNDAYS

Sunday was a horrible day when I was small; I hated it with a passion, but by the time I was a teenager it had improved. There were evening Masses then and I went to evening Mass with my friends, and we wore jeans. Sunday wasn't beginning on Saturday evening as it had done when I was little and my mother had absolute say about how I worshipped.

'Baths, now,' my mother would call out the kitchen window to us as we played. That sharp order she sent us meant the weekend was over. Pleasure was finished. It was the beginning of the slippery slope to Monday morning and another week at school. We trailed indoors. A short time later one little wet girl emerged from the bathroom dressed in her pyjamas. She was under instructions to sit close to the fire and dry her hair. Soon another little girl joined her and another and another, until we were all washed for Mass on Sunday.

When my mother finally emerged from the bathroom struggling under a huge bundle of wet towels, part two of 'getting ready for Mass' began. Part two was ringleting our hair. I pleaded with my mother not to ringlet mine. She ignored me. My hair was very straight. It required the severest ringlets before even the remotest kink could be seen. My mother twirled my hair into sausage shapes. The sausages were tied down with old strips of material. Once this was done I could barely blink. Sleep, too, was impossible. The sausages were released on Sunday mornings. I was supposed to be beautiful by then. I never was.

Sundays were dead. Shops opened for an hour or two, long enough for people to buy the Sunday papers and a carton of cream for the dessert. Sunday was an awkward day. People behaved differently when they wore their Sunday clothes. I couldn't move freely in my Sunday frock and scratchy slip. I had to keep them clean too. The men strolled up and down the gardens in their Sunday suits; they kicked tiny stones with the toes of well-polished shoes. Sometimes they loosened their ties – the nearest they came to ripping off the restrictions imposed by Sunday clothes. They seemed lost too: they had no gardens to dig, no car bonnets to disappear under. No work was permitted on Sundays. Sunday was the Lord's day, the Sabbath; we all had to keep the Sabbath holy. Keeping the Sabbath holy almost drove me mad.

Sundays began with the sound of bells. They pealed every forty-five minutes from early morning to midday. Cortinas, Anglias, and Morris Minors slipped from the same drives, at the same time, every Sunday morning. Families drove to Mass; they parked in the same spot; they knelt in the same pew. Time dragged on Sundays; adults marvelled at how it flew. 'Did you hear so and so prayed for?' they'd ask. 'It can't be a year,' they'd exclaim.

I had a child's prayer book with coloured pictures. What I really wanted was a missal. Adults had missals. Missals were big and black and when they were closed the pages formed an inch of gold or red. I listened at Mass to the missal pages turning. When my parents went to Communion I sat in the pew and leafed through their missals. I fingered the delicate purple and green ribbons the missals had as page marks. I rooted to find the mortuary cards; photographs on the mortuary cards whiled away Mass time for me. I wondered about the people in the pictures who had died long long ago.

I wanted to be holy. Holy people were respected. I wanted to be in on all that. I was worried by the fact the religion made no impact on me. I said my prayers slowly and carefully. I waited for the religious experience to happen. But it didn't. I didn't understand Mass; it was too long. I saw holy people praying at Mass; they sighed, they kept their eyes shut. I tried that but there was no response from the Lord. Clearly he didn't want me to labour in his vineyard. Secretly, I was pleased: religion wasn't attractive. I just thought I should give it a try because everybody said it was very important. Martyrs had died for it. I couldn't see why. If I were persecuted for my religion I wouldn't have put up a struggle. It was so sad and dreary, I would have surrendered it gladly. I used to look at women praying in the church. They all had long sad faces; all the statues of Our Lady looked sad and the Stations of the Cross that lined the church walls were horrible. Our teacher told us Jesus died on the Cross for us, to save us from our sins. But I had done nothing. Jesus and God were so mean: they wanted me to spend my life saying how great they were just because they had done something I never asked them to do. And they spoiled the weekend. They filled Sundays with boredom and rules and restrictions.

During the week I had a role to play. I was a child. I went to school; I did my lessons; I helped Mammy and Daddy and I squeezed in as much fun as I was able. Saturday was my day for fun; I let off steam on Saturdays. Sundays should have been a reprise of Saturdays; but they weren't, all because of religion. Everything was forbidden; everything was a sin. We had to go to Mass. Not to go was a mortal sin. Sunday was a family day; I couldn't call for my friends. I was in enforced captivity with my family and they with me. We fought on the back seat of the car on horrible drives to Glendalough. We sat in the garden unable to move in our Sunday clothes. There wasn't a sound of normal life on Sundays in the garden, no children playing, no lawn mowers whirring. All I could hear was Micheal O'Hehir's voice on the neighbours' transistors.

Mammy went to an early Mass. She didn't think much of later Masses or the people who attended them. Later Masses were frequented by slipshod worshippers. They had been out late drinking on Saturday night. The single people had had dates and gone dancing. According to my mother there was less sanctifying grace available to those who went to later Masses. When I grew a little I went to twelve o'clock Mass with my father. That Mass was packed. We never found seats. My sisters and I fainted and we sat outside on the wall. Some people arrived late to this Mass. The same people left early. My mother was right. I started to leave early myself. My father never noticed. We had to split up to find seats. He never questioned why I was always back at the car before him.

It was mostly teenagers who left Mass early. They gathered around the church and they chatted to their friends. Some really brave ones didn't go into the church at all. I intended joining that group some day. Until then I had to content myself with how much I had accomplished in making my Sundays better. The ringlets and Sunday clothes were gone. While my mother didn't like the later Masses, I was still going; what she didn't know was that by arriving late and leaving at the Consecration I had pared a full half-hour off the time I was spending at Mass. I got up for Mass at the very last minute too: a substantial part of Sunday was over before I was out of bed.

My parents read the Sunday papers. They never got too far into them because they fell asleep. They read the papers in armchairs in winter; in summer they tried to read them in the garden. The summer breezes tugged the pages from their hands and they spent more time chasing big pages around than they spent reading. When I was very young I didn't like newspapers. They were too boring. The worst of all the newspapers I thought then were the *Sunday Times* and the *Observer*. There was even more of them to bore a child. They were huge. One day when I was a teenager I gave them a try. And they changed my Sundays for ever. They rescued me from boredom and inertia. They introduced me to new things. I ignored the vast business and foreign news sections of these papers; I read the book reviews and the colour supplements. And when evening Masses were introduced, my joy knew no bounds. I stayed in bed until Sunday afternoon. When I did get up I passed the day until Mass-time reading my papers.

I never joined the brave band of teenagers who didn't go to Mass. I was a coward. I had a vague notion that when I refused to go to Mass I would tell my parents honestly that I wasn't going any more. I knew they wouldn't accept it from me while I was still a teenager. My little sisters were railing against Mass too. If I stopped going, they'd follow me like a shot; my parents would hold me responsible. Clouds didn't fully lift from my Sundays until I stopped going to Mass.

In primary school we were taught about penal times. I longed to live in a time when Mass was forbidden. When I was a teenager I went to the Aran Islands to learn some Irish. I was staying on Inis Meáin. They didn't have their own priest; a priest came over on Sundays from another island to say Mass. One Sunday he couldn't come: the weather was too bad, they said. It didn't look too bad to me but then I knew nothing of the vagaries of the sea. But the tiny island began to look more attractive. What if I were living there all year round? How many times might I escape Mass during really harsh winter weather? And there would be no mortal sin either!

Today on Sundays I go to town. I meet friends. I browse in bookshops. I sit in coffee shops waiting for my friends. As I wait, I listen to the buskers. I am not living in penal times nor am I living on an island without a priest. I am living in wonderful times, because Sundays have changed.

# 11

## TELEVISION

My mother would pop her head around the livingroom door. She surveyed what she saw in the room with great disapproval; my sisters and I were once again sprawled on the floor watching television. What followed this could vary; if the weather were fine she hooshed us outdoors. She got many years out of expressing horror at the ingratitude of children who could spurn summer sunshine. But the day dawned when we were not so biddable and hours of play in a sunny back garden lost their appeal. She had to change tack; her reproach then became: 'Is there nothing on Teilifís Éireann?' She got great mileage out of that. It lasted all through my childhood and well into my adolescence.

By then my mother had good reason to worry: we had got piped television. We had abandoned Teilifís Éireann for multichannel land. Leaving small children alone in a room where they had unrestricted access to television was quite safe when all they could see was *Daithí Lacha* or *Seoirse agus Beartlaí*. When those children became adolescents with burgeoning sexuality and when they could, with a flick of a switch, see what BBC or ITV had to offer, television became a minefield for mothers.

My parents were slow and reluctant converts to tele-vision. I despaired of them and their radio plays. I felt sure that I would be the butt of every nasty joke at school if it ever got out that Flanagans had no television. I hid this fact as best I could but the talk at school was of little else. At knitting and sewing time clusters of girls huddled together and discussed *The Lucy Show* and *Mr Ed*, the talking horse. I sat with these girls. I pretended I had seen these programmes. I hoped and hoped a misplaced laugh wouldn't blow my cover, or that one of my big-mouthed but honest little sisters might let the terrible secret out.

I took myself off in disgust every evening after school to friends' houses, any friend at all, provided that she had a television. My friends sulked beside me on the couch as I sat spellbound by whatever was on the television. They shoved skipping ropes and dolls under my nose to remind me of the games I'd sworn I would play. My mother was embarrassed by the amount of time I was spending with our neighbours: they would think I had no home to go to. It would reflect badly on her. She gave in, and, on the 23 May 1964, we got a nineteen-inch black-and-white Pye television – and I came home.

Our new television arrived at the weekend; there was nothing on that weekend except golf. Golf from Little Island in Cork. None of us knew the first thing about golf but we sat there watching it anyway, entranced. We arranged 'rabbit's ears', closed the curtains and sat back marvelling at the feathery picture from which we could scarcely pick out the little golfball.

Within weeks I was hooked. I wanted to leave Ireland and move to America. In America I was going to live in a wooden house with a porch swing. My mom would bring me to school in a long station wagon. At 'recess' I would eat from a lunch pail and teachers would sing out 'class dismissed' every two minutes. I wanted a television life, a life just like an episode from *The Donna Reed Show*.

Adults had many scare stories about television. It ruined family life, children's eyesight, homework and reading, but they were just as impressed with it as we were: the sounds from the television reverberated through my bedroom floorboards late at night. Women commented on the continuity girls' clothes. Charles Mitchell was their pin-up and they squealed when they saw Monica Sheridan licking her fingers on her cookery programme.

I lapped television up indiscriminately. The night before my Confirmation my mother called me hundreds of times before I heard her. I was to have my bath. She wanted me to be spotless as I became a strong and perfect soldier of Christ. I was too engrossed in *F Troop* to care. I timed my day around *The Avengers*, *Car 54 Where Are You?*, *Get Smart* and *The Virginian*. My sisters and I sang the theme songs from our favourite programmes. I knew more songs than they did; I was up later and I saw more television. I hummed these tunes as I brushed my teeth or washed the dishes. I loved the accents I was hearing for the first time:

'There's a traffic jam at Harlem that's backed up to Jackson Heights, Car 54 where are you?' I sang that as I swept the floor and Brilloed the pots.

We all loved *Green Acres*, an American comedy which

was on every Saturday evening. On Saturdays three, four, or even five wet little Flanagans sat in front of the fire drying their hair and singing along with Oliver Douglas. Oliver Douglas wanted to try life in the country; his glamorous wife Lisa did not. She floated around the dilapidated kitchen of their ranch house in a feather-trimmed peignoir. 'Green Acres is the place for me,' sang Oliver and the Flanagans:

Farm livin' is the life for me;
Land spreadin' out so far and wide
Keep Manhattan, jus gimme that countryside.

Eva Gabor played the part of Lisa Douglas. Eva Gabor was Hungarian, her accent very strange to our ears. Lisa Douglas sang the second part of the theme song. We joined her too in our best Stillorgan Hungarian accents:

No, New York is where I'd rather stay.
I get allergic smelling hay.
I just adore a penthouse view.
Darling, I love you, just give me Park Avenue.

When I was in sixth class in the primary school my mother thought it might be a good idea if we said the rosary at night. She had tried before to do this but gave up when my father got the giggles. She intended to say it at eight o'clock. We never said the rosary; *The Forsyte Saga* knocked it on the head.

*The Forsyte Saga* was based on the novels of the same name by John Galsworthy. It ran for twenty-six weeks on television. Most adults were addicted to it. I never missed an episode. It introduced me to passion. I discovered a wonderful array of human emotions: sex, lust and adultery.

My parents went out one evening. Granny was staying with us at the time. My granny did not drink tea; she always took Nescafé made with milk. It was my job to make her coffee when my mother wasn't there. I prayed that she wouldn't call for coffee during *The Forsyte Saga*. We watched it together. It was a really good episode. Irene, a beautiful woman, was trapped in a loveless marriage to the wealthy Soames Forsyte. It was said by other Forsyte women over cups of tea that Irene wasn't being 'a wife' to Soames. I couldn't quite grasp what that meant but I figured it was connected to the fact that there was less kissing between Soames and Irene than say Jolyon Forsyte and the German governess. Granny became very uneasy; she tried to engage me in conversation. I was having none of it. She asked me to make her coffee. I sat there simmering. I knew she just wanted me out of the room at a good bit.

The episode was almost over. Granny sensed something horrendous was coming; she wanted me out of the room and fast. I rose to my feet, dawdled to the door, my ears twitched to catch every last bit of the dialogue. 'Mean old thing,' I muttered, 'she's not even thirsty'. I left the livingroom door ajar. I continued to listen: 'Soames decided to exercise his rights as a husband,' a voice said. 'Irene resisted and Soames used force.' What could that be? I wondered as made the coffee in the kitchen. I filed the exact words away in the 'things I will understand when I get older' part of my brain. I brought Granny her coffee. *The Forsyte Saga* was over. Granny sipped in silence. I said nothing. Neither of us ever referred to it again.

Television, not cinema, brought me to films. There were films on almost every day. These films were old. We sat down every Sunday to watch the *Sunday Matinee*. My sisters were addicted to musicals. They loved Judy Garland, Ginger Rogers and Fred Astaire. I hated films where characters suddenly burst into song and millions of women in high-heels and tights took forever to dance down a glass staircase. But I loved baddies. I adored Bette Davis in *The Little Foxes,* especially the lingering shot of her face as she watched her husband die. Chemistry crackled between Spencer Tracy and Katharine Hepburn in polished comedies like *Adam's Rib* and *Pat and Mike.* The Marx Brothers created mayhem and ran rings round an unfortunate society matron, always played by Margaret Dumont. The American films which I saw on television were made when my parents were only tots. If it hadn't been for television, I wouldn't ever have seen them. We just went to the cinema for family treats. The cinemas only had the latest releases: all the James Bond films and the Carry Ons.

Television was expanding, doing bigger and better things. BBC2 began broadcasting. There were films starting on BBC2 on weekend nights at times when the national anthem would have been playing on Teilifís Éireann. I was a teenager when all this came about. I was a moody, introspective mass of phobias then, riven with *Angst* and doubt. I discovered 'gritty Northern dramas' on BBC2 late at night. The landscapes of these films suited my adolescent bleakness: rows and rows of red-brick artisan dwellings, toilets in the backyard, pigeon and whippet rearing. The characters in the 'gritty Northern dramas' were young and angry; they tapped into all I was feeling. Albert Finney, Tom Courteney and Laurence Harvey, they said it all for me.

Laurence Harvey was incredible. He was lean, lithe as a greyhound. He bristled and railed at every slight from 'the top drawer'. He was contemptuous yet vulnerable. He had none of the 'cut-glass' vowels of Anna Neagle or Michael Wilding. The way Laurence Harvey spoke when he played Joe Lampton in *Room at the Top* seemed to cock a snook at all established notions of middle-class stuffiness and convention. I spent most of my adolescence in front of the television. I settled in for a night's viewing after my parents had seen the *Late Late Show* every Saturday night. I would never have been brave enough to face a dance. I existed on a diet of *Sunday, Bloody Sunday*, *Saturday Night and Sunday Morning* and *This Sporting Life*. I do not know what was in the charts then. I can only remember Alan Bates, Tom Courteney, Albert Finney and factory chimneys spewing out smoke over ugly, northern towns.

My parents reproached me for my disloyalty to Teilifís Éireann. There were grand programmes on Teilifís Éireann; why couldn't I was a few of them for a change? My parents and I were destined to disagree about television. Television had come into their lives when their passions and interests were already securely in place; they could exist happily without it. We were ripe for an all-consuming interest. The mere existence of Teilifís Éireann was ample

proof to them that the country was moving along techno-
logically. They would leave avid consumption of its wares
to their children. If what Teilifís Éireann produced was
little more than radio with pictures, my parents wouldn't
have noticed or cared. My sisters and I cut our teeth on
Teilifís Éireann. We were soon hooked on the medium. But
when the BBC and ITV explored the medium's potential
more daringly, our adolescent curiosities dictated that we
should take what they offered us.

I owed nothing to Teilifís Éireann. Teilifís Éireann's
home-produced programmes portrayed a world which I
didn't identify with. I was a child of the suburbs. When I
was growing up, urban Ireland didn't have a voice, it
counted for nothing. To be considered genuinely Irish
then, you had to have a rural background. If you lived in
Dublin, you did so on sufferance. It was very desirable
too to speak Irish, follow the GAA and be as insular as
possible. Teilifís Éireann's programmes were pitched at
that audience – never at someone like me or my sisters.
Angela McNamara, Fergal O'Connor and *Seven Days* left
me cold. I voted with my feet; I went to the other side. I
took my sisters with me. We ignored my mother when she
asked: 'Is there nothing on Teilifís Éireann?'

Our tastes in television programmes inflicted terrible
torture on my father. Because my mother rarely watched
television, it was he who suffered most as our tastes
became more cosmopolitan. He was a simple man. He
liked uncomplicated films and loved Mickey Rooney. He
liked films with a beginning, middle and an end. I made
him sit through Ingmar Bergman and Eric Rohmer as I
went through my foreign phase. He hated subtitles,

nothing ever happened in films with subtitles; all the effort to read the blooming things was a waste of time.

My father's most miserable night of television viewing was the night I decided that we would all watch *Women in Love*. He would gladly have opted for a few subtitles that night. I told my sisters that this would be a really good film. The two names associated with it, Ken Russell and D. H. Lawrence, would guarantee us a great night's sexy viewing. My father couldn't object on moral grounds: some of D. H. Lawrence's novels were on the shelves behind the television. He was a very famous and respected author. We settled ourselves in delighted anticipation of how Russell and Lawrence might thrill us. I was embarrassed by it, not because of anything sexual: it was so full of ridiculous caperings. My sisters were almost asleep; my father grumbled and growled in his chair. My sisters soon woke up when Alan Bates and Oliver Reed began to wrestle naked in front of a roaring fire. But for the fire, the room was in darkness. There was still no mistaking what we saw: two sets of male genitalia bouncing and wobbling up there on screen. 'Is that the time?' asked my father. He squirmed in his chair. He got up and went over to wind the clock. We craned our necks: his new position was spoiling our view. 'If you're staying up to watch the rest of that, make sure the back door is locked.' He scuttled off to bed. Pity about him, I thought. If there were women up there on screen, he mightn't have sloped off so quickly.

It's now over thirty years since I saw my first television. When we got our first set I used to race home from school to see what was on. I hated the wait until 5.30

when the children's programmes began. Sometimes I would turn the set on and sit watching the Teilifís Éireann logo, the St Brigid's Cross. I hated Good Fridays when there was nothing at all on except sad holy music and a static holy picture to accompany it. Now, if I chose, I could watch television twenty-four hours a day. Most households have several sets, there are more channels than I could ever have imagined. I watch very little of it. Television was different when I was a child. It came into my life in the sixties. It blew the cobwebs off my family. It started us asking questions, demanding changes. Inevitably some of its initial power waned, but I could never have envisaged its becoming so bland. Television, which began with such promise, has degenerated into game shows and home shopping, and with the advent of satellite dishes, more of the same is promised.

# 12

## IRISH DANCING

'If you feel like singing, do sing an Irish song.' Leo Maguire wrapped up the *Walton Programme* with those words every Saturday. We ate our dinner on Saturdays with the *Walton Programme* as background music. They played music I didn't like on that programme: 'Deep in Canadian Woods', 'Step Together' and 'Down by the Glenside'. Horrible yucky music; that's all they played.

We ate boiled chicken, mashed potatoes and peas for dinner on Saturdays. I didn't like boiled chicken. Boiled chicken, Leo Maguire and the *Walton Programme* are linked together for ever in my mind with Irish dancing lessons, Irish dancing lessons which I did not want. The fading out of the *Walton* signature tune was our cue to begin scraping the dinner plates and rush to the car if we were to be in time for the dancing lessons.

The lessons were my mother's idea. She had a deep-rooted desire for one of those little girls who suited Irish dancing lessons. Little daughters whose hair would ringlet easily, who would just love to trail from feis to feis, who would carry all their dancing paraphernalia in small weekend cases. But she got me: gauche and without the remotest inclination to dance. I said I didn't want to go. My mother wouldn't listen. I would thank her in years to come, she claimed. When she was my age she would have given her eye teeth to learn to dance. I was going, that was it, end of discussion. My little sisters were coming too. The difference was, they wanted to learn to dance.

The dancing lessons were held in a basement in North Frederick Street. It was dark and dreary and cross-looking old ladies sat at the top of the hall. Some of these women took the money; some taught. There were benches along the sides of the hall where children sat waiting for their lesson. These children were really keen. They copied the others' lessons as they sat. They did all the steps from their sitting positions. Their mothers sat on the benches too, beaming with pride at their daughters' efforts. They knitted to pass the time, their needles clicking while they kept beady eyes on their daughters' rivals out on the floor.

A woman came up to me: 'Did you get a step, love?' she asked me. I didn't understand, but since nobody had said anything to me I assumed that I hadn't. She took me by the arm. She pulled me across the room. 'Heeltoe, heeltoe, heeltoe . . . ' she said as she pulled. I walked after her. 'Heeltoe, heeltoe heeltoe,' she said again. Apparently I was to 'heeltoe, heeltoe, heeltoe' too. This was my 'step'. I followed her across the room. I made a very bad job of it. I could feel her irritation in the way she was holding my arm. My cheeks burned with shame. I was sure my efforts would break a hole in the floor. The little ones on the benches would be laughing at this big new girl who couldn't dance for toffee. The teacher let go my arm. She flung me back to the bench. I wanted to go home right there and then and never come back. But I couldn't. My sisters were 'getting their steps'. They looked as if they were enjoying it too: at least they were showing more promise than I had. Even if I had been free, I couldn't have left: my mother was coming to collect us. None of us knew how to get from North Frederick Street to Stillorgan. I could have throttled my mother for thinking this up, for not listening to me when I said I didn't want to learn to dance. I sat on the bench. There were mousetraps along the skirting boards. The hall was very hot and as I sat counting the mouse droppings tears pricked the backs of my eyes.

A lady who had been sitting on the opposite bench took up a large accordion and began to play. All the pupils joined in the jigs and reels she played. That was the finale. Mammy came down the basement steps beaming at the success of her plan. My little sisters were full of enthusiasm about the dancing lessons. They were going to get dancing costumes, enter the feis and win lots of medals. They jigged their way back to the car. I said nothing.

I told my mother I wasn't going to go back. I told my father too. He said not to make me. My mother said nonsense, I would grow to love the dancing lessons. I knew I wouldn't. I cried. I cried more as the following Saturday drew closer. Then my mother unfolded part two of her plan. She wouldn't bring us dancing that week – or any other week either. She had only brought us the first day so that I could find the way. From the following week

I was bringing my little sisters to the lesson. She had me well and truly cornered.

The sweetest moments were Saturday evening at six o'clock. The dancing lessons were finished. A whole week free of dancing stretched ahead. But the moments, hours and days flew by. By the following Saturday, I was in a state. I bawled my eyes out. My tears plopped into the mashed potatoes and boiled chicken. Leo Maguire was saying, 'If you feel like singing . . . ' while I howled and sobbed. 'I'm not going,' I shouted.

We reached a compromise. I would have to bring my little sisters, but I needn't take any more lessons. I didn't have to stay in the hall either. I could do what I liked for the full two hours the lessons lasted.

For months I explored town while my sisters learned to dance. I had no money, so I was limited to visiting places that didn't involve any expense. I went to Eason's and the Municipal Gallery and I walked up and down Henry Street. I was bored, I would have loved to have some money to spend. But the coins in my pocket were for our bus fare home. I was on a very short leash but anything was better than the dancing lessons.

# 13
—

## CLOTHES

'Maeve Flanagan, are you not going to take off that big top coat?' my teacher asked me, 'You'll melt,' she added. 'I'm fine,' I replied. Wild horses weren't going to get me to part with my coat. It was June, nearly time for summer holidays. The teacher was right; it was a roasting day. One side of the room consisted of windows. The afternoon sun streamed in so we could scarcely keep awake. We squinted at the teacher's writing on the blackboard. She had closed the venetian blinds but only partly; there were bars of sunlight superimposed on whatever she had written. The girls in the class were wearing their summer clothes: cotton dresses and Clark's sandals. The dresses were gorgeous; some had yachts on their skirts; lovely, yellow yachts with sails were printed on the fabric and seagulls soared in the sky above the yachts as they sailed across the navy fabric sea.

I didn't have any summer clothes. I had grown out of last year's clothes; nothing, as yet, had replaced them. I hadn't noticed or minded until the weather got really hot. But the other girls shed their winter layers; they came to school each morning with a fresh summer outfit. The girl beside me asked when was I going to change into my summer clothes. She wasn't trying to be mean. I fobbed her off with something and I went back to my work. I looked around the class. Even if last year's clothes did still fit they could never match the splendour of what I saw in the room. If I had to keep wearing my winter clothes, and I knew I would, more girls would question me. The duffel coat was the answer to my problem. I would keep wearing the winter duffel coat and nobody would see my winter clothes. I would pray that I wouldn't pass out with the heat before we were released for the summer holidays. The duffel coat was warm and woolly. I was almost fully grown. I sweated profusely and probably stank. On the really hot days I opened the pegs of the coat and flapped its halves to flap in a little breeze. I didn't relinquish that coat for anybody.

I was very attached to my duffel coat. I loved it because my mother didn't make it: it came from a shop. It was my blanket of uniformity; other girls had the same coat. When I wore it I looked almost like them. In our primary school we didn't have a uniform. The girls in the school had something different to wear each day. They had startlingly white socks, black patent shoes, cardigans and dresses. All of their clothes came from shops; clothes from shops were what I wanted more than anything else.

Mammy made our clothes. She knitted our jumpers and cardigans. Other mothers sewed too; what they turned out didn't look home-made. These women checked out what was in fashion; they bought patterns and new material. The end result was a source of pride; their daughters were delighted to wear what their mothers created. I was ashamed of what my mother sent me out in. My mother didn't check what was in fashion before she began to dressmake. She didn't consult me on what I would like. She didn't buy patterns. Her levels of competence determined what she made. A pocket on one of her coats was an ugly rectangle of material sewn to the outside of the garment. In shop clothes, pockets were hidden behind a neatly sewn flap. Shop coats like the duffel coat had bone or wooden toggles; they were fastened to the duffle coat by strips of squeaky leather. Buttons on my mother's coats were whatever she found in the sewing basket. She didn't shop for new material either. She cut up old things which she had around the house. Some of my clothes were made from dresses and coats which had been hers originally. The materials were hideously unsuited to their second lives. I had tweed slacks and tweed pinafores and all of them had the woeful buttons too.

Sometimes when I was really unlucky there was enough material left to make a grotesque accessory. A round piece of heavy-duty wool from a man's overcoat might be whipped up into a little bag with drawstrings. An oblong of frieze could reappear as a scarf. I dumped all these accessories behind walls on my way to school. I claimed to have lost them but I couldn't lose the bigger outer garments; they were all I had to cover my nakedness.

I hated the sight of my mother's Singer sewing machine on the kitchen table. I detested the whirring sound it made; I loathed the smell of thread. I dreaded what might emerge when my mother stood me up on a kitchen stool and eased some new monstrosity down over my shoulders and began her pinning and tacking. Even when my mother was making curtains I wasn't safe; some time in the future they could enjoy a second coming – on my back.

I spent a lot of time wishing that I was an only child, the only child of rich parents. Then all my clothes would come from shops. My clothes would be neither home-made nor hand-me-down. Hand-me-down clothes were another source of misery; everything I got to wear came to me via my older sister. If the garment had any life left it went to my smaller sisters after me. I didn't mind what I wore at home or what I wore out playing on the road but I minded very much about what I wore going to school.

My mother was very sneaky about the clothes she made. I told her I didn't like them. I said the girls at school laughed at her dressmaking, saying it was hickey. I thought that might offend her and that she'd stop dressmaking. But she didn't, she told me that the girls at school were secretly jealous of my clothes. Deep down she knew what she made wasn't up to scratch; it was just amateurish making-do. I realised this as my Confirmation approached.

I was given a day off from school. My mother brought me to town and bought me an entire outfit: a yellow suit and blouse, brown shoes and a brown shoulder bag. I got a hat too. I didn't like the hat but girls were supposed to keep their heads covered in the church so I had to give in and wear it.

On the morning of the Confirmation we had to assemble first in the school to have our photographs taken. I usually hated having my photograph taken but that day I didn't care; my Confirmation clothes were lovely. I looked lovely and for the first time in my life, I felt lovely too. The photographer could snap and snap. Daddy wasn't at my Confirmation, because the class he taught was making Confirmation too. Hailstones struck the ground that bitterly cold March day. But nothing could spoil the pleasure I felt in my new yellow suit, which was neither home-made nor hand-me-down.

I was afraid that something might happen to the photographs which were taken at school. If they failed to come out properly, the record of my loveliness would be obliterated. The day after my Confirmation I dressed up again. I ordered my mother to come out to the back garden and take more pictures of me in all my finery. I knew too that my loveliness would be short lived. My Confirmation suit would wear out. I would outgrow it. Given my family's track record on clothes I realised that it would be a very long time before I had anything quite so splendid again. I had no more sacraments to receive; they couldn't be shamed into shopping again. My mother's photographs of me in the garden were my insurance policy against any disaster on the photographer's part. If he didn't fail, the garden pictures still wouldn't be excessive: they'd be double proof that one day I did look nice.

The photographer didn't let me down; my body did. Shortly after my Confirmation it grew. I became taller and broader. Breasts sprouted. I tried to hide them by hunching my shoulders. That didn't work; soon they were full enough to need support. I was fitted for a bra. The bra kept them from flopping and I could move unselfconsciously once more. Putting the bra on at first was complicated until I discovered hooking it at the front, spinning it round and then setting the shoulder straps in place. There was a competition at school to see who was or who wasn't yet wearing a bra. In the middle of lessons a hand would dive under a girl's shoulder blades; the hand checked for the distinctive feel of the band of elastic stretching across the girl's back. Some girls claimed to be wearing bras before they were; this test was designed to root them out. I didn't feel proud of needing a bra; my body's expansion just exacerbated the clothes problem.

My sister's hand-me-downs didn't fit me any more. My mother had at last seen sense and she confined her dressmaking skills to the very young children in the family. Visitors intervened. A female visitor would whisper to me that there was a plastic bag left for me behind the couch. There were a few things in the bag I might like to try on. I was mortified. This was more humiliating than my mother's worst excesses with her sewing-machine. These women had come to visit; they took in my appearance at a glance. They decided it wasn't up to scratch. They would provide the remedy. My mother would expect me to be polite, do as they suggested and try on what cast-offs they brought. They were our guests. I always busied myself with jobs for my mother. I pretended I didn't hear them. I wasn't going to root through their cast-offs, discover they didn't fit and then thank them for their patronage.

There was a light at the end of the tunnel: I was going to secondary school. The secondary school had a uniform. Whether you were a giant or a midget it didn't matter.

The man in Clery's just took your measurements and everything was made up. We went to town again. They measured me for a skirt, a gaberdine and a blazer. The man pulled out a huge drawer and handed us two school jumpers. I hung the uniform up in the wardrobe and I went off to enjoy the summer holidays. I would never again have to worry what I would wear to school.

# 14

---

## SECONDARY SCHOOL

The secondary school didn't look like a school. It was like a rich man's house in a film from the olden days. We left the main road and entered by a very large gate. A drive swept from this gate, curved around the convent hall door and led off to a second gate. The drive curved around an oval lawn and there was a statue of Our Lady in the centre. Added to the side of this large house were several storeys of rooms. These were our classrooms, cloakrooms and hall. Behind all these were basketball courts, tennis courts, an all-weather hockey pitch, paths, fields and flower beds. These led down to the coast road to town. After that was the railway track, the sea and Howth glistening in the morning sun, looking like a lovely island.

We made our way to the hall for assembly. There were tall windows on each side of the hall. There were benches under the windows and girls sat on them chatting, catching up on the summer holiday news. I recognised some girls who had been ahead of me in national school. So this was where they had got to, I thought to myself.

A nun walked into the hall. She carried a tiny hand-bell. She rang it. The girls dispersed into lines. The sixth years stood under the windows on the far side of the hall. They were amazingly tall – women really – and some of them wore nylons. The nun with the bell was the Principal. She went up the steps to the stage and nodded to an old nun who was sitting at the piano. The nun began to play and assembly started with a hymn. The Principal explained to us that over the summer the nuns had changed their names. It was something to do with the Vatican. She called out all the old names and told the gathering what that sister's new name would be. The new names were their own names from childhood. After each name there was a little gasp from some of the girls and a smile or a titter from others.

We didn't have too many classes that first day. I left the school after an hour or so. We would have half-days for the following days to enable us to go to town and queue for books at Greene's of Clare Street. I was allowed to go into to town on my own to shop for my books. As I walked from the school I felt happier than I had ever felt before. My sister wasn't there to spoil it all and she wouldn't be coming. I had my uniform; it fitted me perfectly and everybody was wearing it. The sky was blue as I walked for the bus. A creeper with plummy-coloured leaves partly covered the convent wall and I kicked a spiky green chestnut along the path in front of me. I wanted to keep the chestnut the whole way to the bus-stop but a clumsy kick sent it spinning into the traffic. I was very happy that morning, my first morning in secondary school.

I liked having a different teacher every forty minutes

for each subject. The lay teachers wore gowns and some of them were very young. The English teacher had blond curls, a shiny young girl's face, and she wore a miniskirt which disappeared completely when she sat down. She wore long boots also that went far above her knee. A old tall man taught us Maths. He was very thin and had no cheeks. He had two long lines down his face where his cheeks would have been if his face had any flesh. He filled the blackboard with 'x's and 'y's. Algebra, he called it. I couldn't make head or tail of it and I worried about this. I asked my father; he said not to bother with it, that he never could fathom it either.

French was the best of all. The teacher pulled black curtains across. She worked a projector and little figures appeared on what was just the classroom wall. In the blackness of the classroom and with the aid of the tapes which she played, we could imagine ourselves in Paris. There was a little Eiffel Tower on the wall and in front of it a tiny gendarme spoke to people on the boulevard and a tiny trill on an accordeon created just the right ambience. French was difficult to pronounce: the intonation was a little too dramatic for me to reproduce unselfconsciously in the classroom but in front of the mirror at home I let rip, rolling my 'r's and throwing in a few gallic shrugs for good measure.

Teachers in the secondary school were not cross. Some of them couldn't control us and I felt more impatient with those teachers than I did with the girls who misbehaved on them. Weeks rolled by. Everything was going fine and even if Maths were difficult; French was wonderful and Irish, well Irish was just peasy. The teacher spent class after class going over things we had done hundreds of times, hundreds of years ago, in the national school. We had school on Saturdays until lunchtime and I didn't mind the very short weekend in the least, I would have quite happily gone to school on Sundays as well. My first year flew. I discarded my knee socks, didn't wear nylons but wore tights. I also stopped wearing my plaits.

Some girls in the school were terribly smart. Not clever at their books smart: they were that too but they had style as well. There was a certain number of them in each year and they could easily be identified by someone like me who lacked their attributes. They had fine brains but they didn't grow white-faced and anxious about examinations; they never twitched nervously as they watched for others who could rival their marks at tests. They were great fun and never looked down their noses at others who didn't quite have their style. They didn't seem aware of their own dazzle at all. I was never one of them, I didn't long to be either but I watched them in fascination.

Smart girls didn't fasten the belts of their gaberdines around their waists, buckles to the front, as the House of Clery's intended them to be worn. They fastened the belt to the back of the gaberdine. There it lay, like a half-belt, permanently closed. Worn like that, pulled tightly back, it emphasised the girl's womanly shape. Worn as the nuns, our mothers and Clery's intended, the wearers looked like a cross between a letterbox and a haystack. They took off their hoods too. If it rained they used umbrellas. Long hair flowed down their backs and if it was too wavy they ironed it.They used eggs and vinegar when they washed their hair. None of the smart girls used schoolbags; they slung canvas bags over their shoulders. These they had bought in camping shops and Army surplus stores in Liffey Street and Capel Street.The bags were covered with the names of the groups they followed. They didn't believe in copies either; they had folders which had pictures of Fidel Castro, Che Guevara, and sometimes Jesus pasted on to the covers. Smart girls went out with boys who rode motorbikes and wore Army greatcoats. The shopped in the Dandelion Market and they didn't go to Mass. These girls were angry, angry about the world and its inequalities. Their favourite word was 'why?' They were unconcerned about exam results. Two honours would get them into Arts, so why cram? They fully intended to study Arts too and get involved in student politics as soon as possible. Exams, they declared loudly and frequently, were inherently corrupt, a product of the rotten bourgeois system. Smart girls in our school came to life in religion class.

The year we were doing our Inter Cert we had a middle-aged nun teaching us religion. One day she told us the story of poor little Maria Goretti, how she was raped and murdered and of the final repentance of her attacker. She shouldn't have resisted, interjected one of these girls. If she had let him have sex with her she would have lived, she continued. She wouldn't be a virgin any longer but at least she would be alive. It was a point our teacher conceded. She had warned us to accept nothing at face value, to think it out for ourselves and come to our own conclusions. She didn't seem to feel hoist with her own petard. The class continued, discussing the smart girls' theory, unearthing others too, in the process, who didn't prize purity above life. It was a time for questioning and protesting. Bobby Kennedy and Martin Luther King were not long dead, the Berrigan Brothers were leading anti-Vietnam demonstrations and the Troubles had begun in the North. Angry young women were acceptable ... Bernadette Devlin had just slapped Reginald Maudling.

Sometimes I talked about these religion classes at home. My parents were amazed by my accounts of our discussions. They didn't mind but they asked me did we ever learn a few psalms or read the Gospels. I had a Bible somewhere but it was as clean as the day I bought it. I stopped bringing it to school and tuned in daily to the discussions instead. I told my parents that we had no time left for the Bible or the Psalms: 'We have too much to consider. We move from the particular to the general; we can say what we like so long as there's no flaw in the logic of our thought.' They didn't ask me any more.

The assemblies changed format. The old nun and her piano were dispensed with. No more 'Tantum Ergo' or 'Soul of My Saviour'. Two sixth years with guitars took the hymns at assembly and new hymn sheets were printed. 'Hello Darkness, My Old Friend' we sang after that, or 'Like a Bridge over Troubled Waters I Will Lay Me Down'. The sixth years who played the guitars had two long curtains of hair almost covering their faces; their noses just peeped out through these curtains and they attached the guitars to their shoulders with a multi-coloured *crios*. I thought they were Dublin's answer to Joan Baez.

Abandoning the traditional hymns had some bizarre and comical results. The assembly hall had a gallery. My

rang for the nuns, smells of cabbage drifted from the kitchen, clouds of steam belched across the cloakroom windows from the convent laundry. The choirs rehearsed in the hall and that sounded really beautiful from my vantage point in the cloakroom. I decided to sneak in and join the choir classes when I was mitching the games class.

It was only a matter of time before I was discovered in the cloakroom; cloakrooms and toilets were very obvious places to look for mitching girls. I didn't want my parents to discover what I was doing. The only tiny thing in my favour was that I wasn't the type of girl who might be thought likely to mitch. Even if I were discovered and my parents were informed, I wasn't going back. I would fight them tooth and nail on this one if it came to it. I wasn't ever attending a hockey, basketball, or gym class. I was finished with anything which involved wearing those tiny divided skirts or made me feel foolish.

I joined the back of the choir classes. I went to choir two and three times a week and was never discovered because two and three classes had choir at the same time. The hockey mistress never seemed to miss 'Glawses' and I forgot about her as I slipped into the back row of the seconds who didn't know me from Adam. And, that first day, they were beginning something I liked: 'Blow The Wind Southerly'. I had heard Kathleen Ferrier singing it on the radio at home. 'They told me last night there were ships in the offing/ and I hurried down to the deep rolling sea.' Lovely – it beat the socks off 'Bully one, bully two, bully three.'

'Sing it too 'loo' first girls,' said the choir mistress. I

sang it to 'loo' as well and never went to a games class again.

The years in secondary school flew by. There were only five of them, compared to eight in national school. They flew too because I was older, coming closer to the age-group that always claims time flies, and I was much happier. For three full years I was in a place where nobody else from my family was known. I was judged for myself alone. My next youngest sister started in the secondary school when I was in fifth year and the following year another little sister came too. They didn't impinge on my life at all; the school was huge and we hardly ever saw one another. My year group would have seemed like grown women to them, just as the fifth and sixth years seemed to me when I was their age. I saw them in the distance, though, with their own pals, lost in skirts which were too long and gaberdines which could easily have fitted two girls.

One afternoon all the sixth years were brought to-gether. It was just before the Leaving Cert. We were given tea and fluffy biscuits in the refectory. We stuffed ourselves on Mikados, Kimberleys and Coconut Creams. Two young nuns were brought in to speak to us. They were only a year or two older than us, though we hadn't seen that initially. They were wearing habits so I had assumed they too were at least a hundred and five like all the other nuns. They were postulants. They had felt the call to the religious life when they were just our age, finishing school. They were there to talk to us about the likelihood that some of our sixth years were feeling the same. They were fresh-faced, had guitars and seemed genuinely happy. It was a big no-no with the smart girls, of course. Out of the question with the girls who went to the dances in Belfield every Saturday night and covered their love-bites with make-up before school on Monday. Others were too deeply into the Hare Krishnas to consider Catholicism in any shape or form. It hadn't entered anybody's head to consider the religious life. We finished the biscuits and tea, tickled pink that the order might be so desperate as to want any of us. I had been very happy in secondary school but never so happy as to consider entering the convent. When I left school after the last exam in the Leaving Cert, the convent chapter was definitely closed.

## 15

### LEAVING HOME

There were no secondary schools in the small country places where my mother and father grew up. They travelled far away from home for secondary education. They left home at twelve, returning thereafter just for holidays. Life had changed; they were visitors rather than full family members. The tiny ins-and-outs of the family's daily lives were mysteries to them; they were virtual strangers to their youngest siblings.

My father was in boarding school during some of the war years. Food was scarce; he was often cold. He dreamed of home and the holidays. He dreaded bad weather which might delay his crossing home to Aran and his family. He prayed for bad weather at the end of the holidays, bad weather that would lengthen his stay at home. His wish was rarely granted.

My parents came to Dublin for further education and work. They had digs on South Circular Road; that's how they met. The houses of the South Circular Road were full of young men and women from every part of rural Ireland. My parents married and moved to Stillorgan. Stillorgan was miles out from the city; nobody knew a thing about it. They chose it because the new houses there suited a tight 1950s budget. Stillorgan was also on the Harcourt Street line; my father could travel to school on the train. Nobody had a car then.

Our neighbours' backgrounds were exactly the same. They too had origins in some part of rural Ireland. Their brothers still farmed the family holding. They had also come to Dublin for education and work. The women had resigned from their jobs on marriage. Whether they wanted to or not, they became full-time mothers and housewives. The men commuted to town every morning. Most of them were civil servants. They still had the strong accents of their homeplaces.

These people didn't think much of Dublin. Dublin wasn't 'home.' Dublin was somewhere they had migrated to. It was tolerated. They were suspicious of Dublin accents. You could speak unintelligibly provided it was in a country accent. A Dublin accent marked you out as 'common.' There was something almost fly-by-night about a Dublin accent.

My mother was reared on a farm. Her parents came to visit every May. May was chosen because they could also take in the Spring Show. They always brought huge sacks of potatoes, heads of cabbage and enormous carrots. We children had to be fattened up. Poor little ones growing up in the city where there wasn't a decent vegetable to be found. My grandfather fled as soon as the Spring Show was over. He couldn't bear the city, the noise, the traffic or the sense that everyone was living on top of everyone else. And, although my grandmother stayed

on for a few weeks, she shared her husband's views on
life in the city. She used to stand at our kitchen window
staring out at our narrow strip of garden. This was all the
land her daughter and her daughter's daughters owned.
She shivered as she contemplated that fact.

I didn't like any negative comments about Dublin.
Dublin was my home; I loved it. People who criticised
Dubin had no manners. When I visited the country I never
passed any uncomplimentary remarks. I kept all my
negative views on country life to myself. The countryside
was beautiful, especially in summer, but it was too quiet.
There were no shops; they only had RTE on the telly. I
hated being left there on my own. I would sob my heart
out as I watched my parents' car grow smaller as they
went up the lane from my grandparents' house and left
me to stay on for a visit I didn't want to make. There
wouldn't be anything to keep me company; there wouldn't
be a single sound to listen to, except the kitchen clock
ticking on the dresser as I counted the hours left until I
could go home.

A day trip to the country wasn't too bad. Before I had
time to get bored it was over. Our car was at the top of
the lane waiting to join the traffic on the Dublin road. The
intense blackness of the country would slip by quickly;
soon we would see the lights on the outskirts of Dublin.
I loved getting back to Dublin. I loved to see the news-
agents' shops open late and all the chip shops doing a
roaring trade. The papers swirling on the streets were ugly
and dirty but it was home. There were no calves staring
out over walls at me, following me with big eyes and
lowing pitifully.

Mammy and Daddy said we were very lucky to be living in Dublin: we would never have to leave home for schooling. We were spoiled for choice as regards schools – all within walking distance. Two universities were a short hop on a bus from our house. There was even a teacher training college nearby if anyone of us 'got the call'. I agreed with my parents, but for different reasons. I liked living in the capital city because all the best and most exciting things were there. We had an airport, buses to take us everywhere, shopping centres which opened late, and a vast choice of theatres and cinemas. If I were living in the country I would be very lucky if my father took me to the cinema on the back of the tractor once in a blue moon.

But there was one time in the year that I would have liked not to be from Dublin. On the days we broke for school holidays I would have liked to have been a boarder in a Dublin school. Heading home to a remote part of the country would have increased the joy of getting holidays. It would have made Christmas seem more festive. I based this on my father's stories of going home for Christmas. There would be great excitement about my imminent arrival. I would be a visitor; they would treat me with respect and there would be fancy things bought from the shops. Being from Dublin meant that there was no magic to going home, no drama to arriving. When the school closed I just hopped on my bicycle, pedalled for ten minutes and there I was 'home.' Instead of being met at a station on a frosty winter's night with hugs, kisses and a few tears, my mother told me to change out of my uniform quickly. She issued me with a plastic bucket of warm sudsy water and sent me off to clean the venetian blinds. I tried to convince myself that these anti-climactic homecomings were a small price to pay for the sophistication I possessed by being a native of the capital city.

Throughout childhood, leaving home was a vague, remote concept. I accepted without question what my parents said of the miseries and hardships involved. My parents invited cousins who were studying in Dublin to the house so that they wouldn't spent lonely weekends in bedsits in Ranelagh and Rathmines. We were so lucky compared to the visitors, my parents claimed; we would never have to leave home. We could stay with Mammy and Daddy for ever and ever.

I never imagined differing sharply with my parents on this subject. When I started to go to university it hit me like a thunderbolt that living in Dublin was a bit of serious bad luck. At university I met young fellows and girls of my age who were already left home. In first year they were staying in hostels run by nuns or in digs. There was nothing to envy when that was their living accommodation. There was plenty to envy, though, when we all went into second year.

These same students left the hostels and digs; they went into flats. Their parents consented to the new living arrangements: they had proved that they could spend a year in the city without going off the rails; they had passed their exams and balanced their budgets.

Nothing in my life changed as a result of going to university. University was just a little bit further up the road from the secondary. I cycled to secondary school; I studied in my small bedroom. I cycled to university too and I studied in the same bedroom. I didn't expect my life to change by going to university. But when I saw how much life had changed for country students I wanted mine to change as well. When I saw the students in second year installed in their bedsits I didn't see the grottiness or consider the expense. I saw freedom; freedom they had and which I didn't. They could skip lectures, get drunk, eat sensibly or not eat at all. All of this could happen far away from their mammy and daddy's prying eyes. They didn't seem to be pining away for their families either; they flourished.

They rolled up the landlord's rubberbacked carpet, covered his leatherette suites with throws and his flowery wallpaper with posters. They gave parties. Parties went on all night. I was never there when the parties ended: I was long gone to catch the last 46A to Stillorgan. I had drawn a very short straw. My smug confidence that I was inherently sophisticated by being from the city was taking a severe dent, as I rushed from parties like a little child and raced like some poor Cinderella from the ball. They were free to discuss and put the world to rights until dawn if they chose. They would sit on the floor of their flats, sipping Hirondelle and eating chilli con carne, while I was reporting in to my parents. I felt very aggrieved – especially as my parents had spent so much time vaunting my good fortune.

And I knew the situation wouldn't necessarily improve when I was working: most jobs were in Dublin. I wanted to stay there myself. If Mammy and Daddy lived to be ninety-nine would I still be with them?

Some of the neighbours' sons and daughters had

begun to work. They wore businessy clothes and commuted to their jobs from the parents' homes. I did
likewise. Only one girl I knew left home. She wanted to
be independent. Her mother said as much candidly to the
neighbours. Mother and daughter remained on excellent
terms: it could be done. My mother and all the other
mothers took a dim view of the girl's move. The girl was
artistic: that went most of the way to explaining her odd
behaviour. I knew the road ahead would be rocky.

In our family leaving home was viewed as a kind of
betrayal. My sisters were engaged; they would be leaving.
Leaving for marriage was tolerated; marriage was a
respectable institution. Leaving home just for freedom
and independence was capricious. It was spurning a
perfectly good home. It smacked, too, of something
vaguely indecent. What could a well-brought-up girl want
to do so badly that she had to be miles and miles away
from her mammy and daddy to do it?

I made my decision: I was going. Shortly after my
sisters' weddings I would also be gone. The shock of three
leaving could be borne as easily as two. I would appeal
to my parents' sensible streak. I wouldn't go into a flat; I
would buy a house. I began to save furiously on the quiet.
I lay on my bed looking at auctioneers' handouts. I stared
and stared at my building society account book, willing
it to grow. I bought some household items and I stored
them in the bottom of the wardrobe. My father called my
little store my 'running-away kit.' He suggested I bring my
single bed with me. My mother glowered at him for aiding
and abetting me.

I left home embarrassingly late. My mother and father

had their daughters under their roof for far longer than their parents or grandparents. They had us there for so long they feared what might happen after we'd gone. What would they fill the space with? Filling the space wasn't my problem; it wasn't my sisters' problem either. For a girl from Dublin, leaving home was a complex business.

# 16

## THE FUNERAL

Evening traffic crawled along the dual carriageway. The rain fell heavily. The shopping centre, brightly lit for Christmas, was busy. Across the road from it was the hospital mortuary and I was standing in its yard. Four hearses were parked there, their tailgates open to the dark sky. Inside in the chapel I heard voices murmuring prayers for the dead. Those prayers were not for my father. I had been in the chapel for them but then I left. I had to: it was too crowded; with so many funerals happening at almost the same time, it was difficult to decide which one to join. Each coffin was behind a curtained cubicle. The mortuary walls were covered with white tiles, the lids of the coffins were resting against them. The place was like a butcher's shop. And the dead man didn't look like my father: he was too small, shrunken already. He wasn't wearing his glasses.

I preferred standing outside. It was still drizzling. Mourners crowded in groups in the yard. Some of them spoke to me. Others stood apart chatting. Their cigarette butts glowed in the darkness. I joined the edge of the group of mourners, half-listening to what they said. I focused my full attention on the traffic flowing from the city. It was heavy, scarcely moving. I counted sets of headlights. The car tyres sizzled in the rain. I would have to go back inside again before they closed the coffin. But I didn't want to just then. I tired of counting headlights. I started on brakelights; that was more challenging. I had to crane my neck to see them. There were fewer of them in the citybound traffic. They formed a blurry red cortège snaking its way towards the city.

Two days earlier, I had been woken by the sound of the telephone ringing. It was Saturday, not yet seven o'clock. There had to be a mistake: nobody could want me that urgently to call so early. I tried to snuggle back deeper into the duvet but the phone rang and rang. When I did answer, it was my sister Róisín. 'Daddy's dead,' she said. Her words hurt my ears like a sudden scald. I put down the phone. I had got it all wrong; she hadn't called. I rang back. It was true. I sat on the couch, still wearing my nightclothes. It was too early to ring friends. I felt cold. I lit a huge fire in the sittingroom and put on my anorak. Still I could not get warm. I wanted to go to work. I wanted it to be a normal day. I would have welcomed a day at school answering silly queries about the date and what page we were supposed to be on.

There were carrier bags on the armchair. I had begun some Christmas shopping. Somewhere in one of the bags was a Swiss army knife for my father. I filled the washing machine. I hoovered the house from top to bottom. It was still too early to ring my friends. I made tea and some toast and sat on the couch to have some breakfast.

After the phone calls I went to my parents' house. My mother wasn't there. She had gone to the undertakers. The Christmas tree was in the hall. The big clock was gone from the livingroom mantelpiece. My mother took it away every Christmas to make room for the little crib. There were scissors and Sellotape on the floor. People had begun to call. We had plenty to give them to eat and drink. The house was groaning under the weight of Christmas food and drink. Our callers sat down. They nibbled mince pies and sipped whiskey. Suddenly, someone would remember why they had come and start to cry. My mother hadn't returned. I left the livingroom and went upstairs. Everything was as it always was. I went into my parents' bedroom.

There were no signs that my father had died there just a few hours earlier. Ambulance men had carried him down the stairs on the stretcher. He was already dead by then. My mother insisted that he be taken to hospital anyway. Maybe there, they might have something which could resuscitate him. The room was quiet; there were no signs of all that panic. I sat on my father's side of the bed. Little stacks of coins were piled on the locker. My father emptied his pockets before he undressed and put the loose change on the locker. When we were young, we helped ourselves to it the following morning for copies and bus fares. His cheque book was there too, with some cheques already filled in for January's bills, all written in his perfect, neat handwriting.

Someone tugged at my sleeve. It was my aunt. 'They're closing the coffin now,' she said. I went in again for a last look and came out immediately. The hearse was backed nearer to the door. Its engine idled as the undertakers' men slid my father's coffin in. Exhaust fumes filled the air. Wreaths were lined up on both sides of the coffin; their ferny green scents mingled with the exhaust fumes. The hearse moved off slowly; we came behind in a big black car. The traffic lights were red. The hearse waited to enter the dual carriageway and we waited behind it. Traffic was still streaming from the city. The service station on the dual carriageway was a blaze of Christmas lights. A gigantic Santa Claus was painted across the plate-glass window. 'Ho, ho, ho,' bubbled from his mouth as his team of reindeers whooshed him across the glassy landscape. The lights turned to green. The hearse slipped into the dual carriageway; we followed it to our parish church.